Eve Lockett studied English and Fine Art at Exeter University, graduating in 1979. Her creative writing has included stories, poetry, lyrics, and short drama sketches, some for radio. For eight years she worked with a Christian mission agency, producing and editing their publicity material—newssheets and audio-visuals. Eve was licensed as a lay reader in 1997, married and moved to Oxfordshire. For some years she has helped with an after-school club, involving regular biblical storytelling. She received a diploma in Biblical and Theological Studies from Wycliffe Hall in 2001.

Text copyright © Eve Lockett 2005
The author asserts the moral right
to be identified as the author of this work

Published by
The Bible Reading Fellowship
First Floor, Elsfield Hall
15–17 Elsfield Way, Oxford OX2 8FG

ISBN 1 84101 366 8
First published 2005
10 9 8 7 6 5 4 3 2 1 0
All rights reserved

Acknowledgments
Unless otherwise stated, scripture quotations are taken from the
Contemporary English Version of the Bible published by HarperCollins
Publishers, copyright © 1991, 1992, 1995 American Bible Society.

A catalogue record for this book is available from the British Library

Printed in Singapore by Craft Print International Ltd

TALES
of Grace

50 five-minute stories
for all-age talks, sermons
and assemblies

Eve Lockett

For David, and for my mother

ACKNOWLEDGMENT

Thank you to all those who helped me in researching subjects as diverse as wildebeest, bell-ringing, lodestones and computer viruses. Thank you to those of you who encouraged me by your prayers, comments, enthusiasm and willingness to listen to yet another story. Special thanks to Jan Osborne, to Dianne Rees, and to David Lockett, for your guidance, encouragement and wisdom.

CONTENTS

TALES OF GUIDANCE

TALES OF TRUST

FOREWORD

When I was a boy, my grandmother introduced me to all kinds of stories. I would stay at her house every other weekend or so, and she would fill me with fizzy drinks, let me stay up way past my bedtime and watch scary stories with her on the telly. That is, after all, what grandmothers are for! And then, on Sunday morning, she would drag me out of bed, take me to church and tell me Bible stories—because my grandmother was also my Sunday school teacher. And that, after all, is what Sunday school teachers are for!

But there were other stories, too. When I got a little older, she bought me a book all about those pesky 'birds and bees'. This was a great help, as it turns out, because the sum total of knowledge passed on to my brothers and me by our father went something like this: 'Boys, you know when you go into a shop and you drop something and break it. You have to pay for it, right? Well, it's like that with girls.' Hmm.

There was nothing in grandma's book about shops. Well, not that book anyway. But there was another book, filled with other kinds of stories, one of which I have never forgotten. It was called *The Lie in Believe* and it was all about a little girl who was so honest that when she did finally fib everyone believed her anyway. As you can imagine, this turned into a bit of a habit, until, like the Boy Who Cried Wolf, she was eventually caught out. Maybe it was the clever title. Maybe it was the point of the story. Maybe it was the way it was told. But that little moral tale has always stuck with me.

I think that's the way these kinds of stories work. They grab your attention. They make their point, quickly and powerfully. And they have a positive effect long after the story has ended. That's what Eve Lockett is up to in this collection, and hopefully, her stories will have that effect on you and the children with whom you share them.

Bob Hartman

✣

INTRODUCTION

Storytelling has become extremely popular over recent years. Many towns and cities have storytelling clubs where people can develop their skills in a friendly and encouraging setting. There is a growing number of Christian storytellers, telling stories from the Bible or stories with a Christian theme. They find people willing to listen who might never otherwise attend a church service or hear a sermon.

The power of storytelling is in stirring people to respond, to think, to act, in ways that abstract lessons often fail to do. Stories help us to see from different angles, they free us to explore our own feelings and beliefs, they engage our emotions as well as our minds, they speak to adults and children alike and they connect us with each other.

The stories in this book are intended to tease out biblical truths. The themes that they illustrate are some of the main themes of the Christian life, such as grace, forgiveness, trust and prayer. They are strongly linked in each case to Bible passages, so that study and storytelling complement each other.

Where can they be used?

The stories are suitable for use in a variety of settings: in church services; in the children's talk before the adult sermon or during a family service; in school assemblies and after-school clubs; in Sunday clubs; as material for meditation; as bedtime or family reading.

Who are they for?

They are written with both children and adults in mind, and can be used with only children present, only adults present, or with a mixed-age group. Some have a more traditional flavour, others a contemporary setting.

Are they for reading or telling?

You may prefer to read the stories out loud or to tell them. Telling does not mean learning off by heart, it means making the story one's own. Telling requires some preparation, dwelling on the story, identifying the elements that hold it together and the main points that need making, and then relating it in your own words. The effect can be more immediate and powerful than reading.

However, children and adults love being read to as well as being told stories, so the choice is yours.

The use of Bible references

Bible references have been selected from a wide range of books from the Old and New Testament. A key verse from the Contemporary English Version has been given to help focus the theme of the story.

The use of sermon pointers

The sermon pointers are written as questions, in order to stimulate rather than prescribe. They can be used for sermons or for further discussion or personal study.

Discussing the stories with children

The questions for younger listeners are given as suggestions. Starting with a simple question helps to get the children used to answering, and the ideal is to move into a discussion rather than a question-and-answer session.

Use of visual aids and actions

The visual aids and actions are provided to set the scene before the story begins, or to give some visual reference during the story. They also help to gain the children's attention, but older members of the congregation can be included where appropriate. Again they are given as suggestions, and you may well have the perfect visual aid at home which you would prefer to use.

And in conclusion...

Try pacing the story; don't rush it. Allow time for the story to sink in, and for children and adults to think of the comments they really want to make. The creativity of stories is that they lead us to unexpected places. Some wonderful treasure may be uncovered in the process.

THE POOR THIEF

Once there were three friends—a fox, a hare and a badger—and they found some treasure buried in a man's field. He was a good man, and always kind to the animals, but because they were greedy they stole his treasure and ran off with it into the woods.

Time passed, and the fox and the badger grew very rich, making a lot more money and buying fine houses and fine furniture. But the hare was not so fortunate. Gradually he became poorer and sadder, and began to think his life was over.

Now it so happened that the fox and the badger, who were still friends, were one day passing the house of the man they had robbed. But it was all so long ago that they had forgotten it.

They reached a beautiful picnic spot on the edge of an escarpment, looking out over the hills. There they opened their picnic hamper. Inside was the most wonderful feast, which they spread out on a white cloth. As they were eating, the fox said, 'Did you hear something?' At exactly the same time, the badger said, 'What was that?' Someone was calling for help, and the voice seemed to be coming from way below them.

They looked over the edge of the cliff, and there, lying wounded on an outcrop of rock, was the hare.

'Do you see that fellow?' said the badger. 'Isn't it…?'

'Poor old hare!' said the fox. 'What a mess he's made of his life!'

'We should help him,' said the badger. 'Here, let's hang the tablecloth over the edge and he can climb up.'

'How thoughtful you are,' said the fox, and so they dangled the cloth down towards the hare. But, however hard he tried, he could not reach it.

'Oh, friends,' he cried. 'Please, couldn't you find a rope?'

'We don't have a rope,' said the fox.

'Can't you ask the man in the house for one?'

'I hardly think,' laughed the badger, 'that an important person like that would lend us a rope to rescue you. What were you doing to fall over the edge?'

'I... I was weak. I must have fainted, and then I found I was falling.'

'It's your own fault, you know,' said the fox. 'You don't look after yourself.'

The poor hare began to cry piteously.

'Better leave him, I think,' said the badger. 'He's had a sad life. And you know, at the end of the day, he's only a poor thief.'

At that moment, a young man came walking up to the edge of the cliff. The fox and the badger drew back rather nervously, and asked him who he was.

'I live up at the house,' explained the young man. 'My father heard someone crying for help and he sent me to see who it was.'

He looked over the edge and, directly he saw the hare, he began climbing down the cliff face.

'What are you doing?' cried the badger.

'I'm rescuing him,' said the young man. He reached the ledge, picked up the poor hare, and put him inside his jacket before starting to climb up again.

'You foolish man, you'll be killed!' called the fox. 'And what you don't know is, that hare is a thief!'

'Yes, I do know,' replied the young man, and he looked at the badger and the fox as if to say, '... and I know you're thieves too'. They were so indignant, and so frightened, that they ran away quickly and went back to their city life.

'I'm sorry I stole from you,' said the hare in a small voice from inside the man's jacket.

'That's all right,' said the young man. 'Here, you're safe now.' And he put the hare gently down on to firm ground. 'I think you'd better come back with me to the house and we'll have something to eat.'

And so they did.

> **'I came to invite sinners.'** MARK 2:17

BIBLE REFERENCES

Psalm 51; Mark 2:15–17; Romans 5:6–21; Galatians 1:3–5

SERMON POINTERS

✴ **Psalm 51:** How does the writer of this psalm view God? Do we have the same trust and confidence in God? What is the writer's attitude towards himself?

✴ **Mark 2:15–17:** What disturbed the Pharisees about Jesus? How did Jesus see his own work?

✴ **Romans 5:6–21:** How is God's kindness shown towards those who are sinful? What is the result of Adam's sinfulness? What is the result of the coming of Christ?

✴ **Galatians 1:3–5:** How are God the Father and Jesus Christ seen as united in purpose? How did Christ rescue us?

QUESTIONS FOR YOUNGER LISTENERS

✴ Which of the three friends did nothing wrong?

✴ Which needed most help? Did the other two try their best to help?

✴ Why did the fox and badger run back to the city?

✴ Why did the young man help the hare?

✴ How does God help us in the same way?

VISUAL AIDS AND ACTIONS

⋆ A picnic hamper
⋆ A white tablecloth

Use the tablecloth as it appears in different points in the story.

❖

THE UPSIDE-DOWN TREE

Once there were three trees—a maple, a cherry and a fig tree—and they grew together in the corner of a great garden. Now the garden had become so overgrown that the trees struggled to see the sunlight.

'I shall grow upwards till I am taller than all the other trees,' said the maple. 'Then I shall have as much sunshine as I need.'

'I shall grow in all directions,' said the cherry. 'I am bound to find patches of sunlight if I struggle along far enough.'

But the fig tree had a plan that he didn't want the others to know. He decided to grow downwards through the earth and out the other side. He had been told that on the other side of the world the sun shines all night long.

So the maple held herself very straight and tall and concentrated on growing upwards, and the cherry wildly began putting out shoots and branches in all directions. Both of them felt that they were doing rather well and, although they only grew a little closer to the sun, they thought it was worth it. But the fig tree waited till it was night-time and then burrowed down and down into the soil. All his leaves and branches began to protest. 'We're not made for going under-ground,' they said. 'We'll wither and die in the dark.'

'It's for your own good,' said the fig tree. 'Wait till you see the wonderful land where the sun shines all night.'

'We'll never live to see it,' cried the leaves. 'We can feel ourselves dropping off already.'

Down and down went the tree, and the deeper he went, the weaker he grew. 'Perhaps this wasn't such a good idea,' he thought. 'I'm never going to make it.'

But he didn't say anything because he didn't want to admit he'd made a mistake.

'Please turn back,' begged one of the branches. 'We're starving down here.'

'Nonsense!' replied the fig tree. 'You will see the sun very soon if you just do what I say.'

But, for all his brave words, the tree had begun to slow down and he was soon too weak to move at all.

'Help!' he thought. 'Help! I can't go any further!' He gathered his branches around him and lay there under the ground, very still.

But then he heard a noise coming from far above him, and he knew he'd heard it before. It was the sound of someone digging. The digging went on and on, though sometimes there were pauses and the clink of a teacup.

'Ow!' said the tree, as a metal spade hit him in the side. Then a rope was passed under him and he was hauled back up into the fresh air.

'You were growing the wrong way,' said a voice. 'It's a good thing I found you.'

The fig tree felt battered and exhausted, and he leant against the wall behind him. He noticed that many of the trees and bushes around him had been pruned and cut back, so that all of them now had enough sunlight.

It was not long before his leaves grew again, and he felt much stronger. As the years passed, he grew taller and taller, and gave beautiful fruit. But for the rest of his life, he never forgot the day the gardener found him.

> 'The Son of Man came to look for and to save people who are lost.' LUKE 19:10

BIBLE REFERENCES

Psalm 139:7–12; Luke 15:1–7; Luke 19:10; Colossians 1:12–14

SERMON POINTERS

✳ **Psalm 139:7–12:** Are these comforting words or disturbing ones? Why would anyone try to escape from God's Spirit? How is this a description of grace?

✳ **Luke 15:1–7:** Why did Jesus tell this story with the Pharisees listening? In our churches, do we focus mainly on the lost sheep or the 99 others?

✳ **Luke 19:10:** Are all people lost, or only those whose lives are in a mess? How did Jesus show in his life that he was looking for the lost?

✳ **Colossians 1:12–14:** Are we grateful that God has rescued us? What has he rescued us from? What has he brought us into?

QUESTIONS FOR YOUNGER LISTENERS

✳ Why did the tree try to grow through to the other side of the world?

✳ Did he have the wrong idea of what it would be like there?

✳ Why didn't he turn round and go back?

✳ What did the gardener do to help the trees? Did he care about them?

✳ How does God help us to go the right way?

VISUAL AIDS AND ACTIONS

✳ Some gardening tools—gloves, pruning shears, spade and so on. Maybe bring them in a wheelbarrow.

Ask the children why plants need light.

THE GIFT

Many thousands of years ago, the king of a great land learnt that all the people and the animals in his kingdom were facing many difficulties. So he sent his messenger to meet with them on the side of a high hill to talk with them. The messenger looked out over the hillside at the crowd gathered below. One by one the people stepped forward and told their stories.

'The river is full of chemicals and I can't drink from it,' said the deer.

'I'm cold and I have no shoes,' said the little girl.

'My brothers are kept in a cage,' said the wolf.

'I carry men into battle,' said the horse. 'And I carry them out dead.'

'I am forced to pay for the crops I grow,' said the farmer. 'And I can't feed my family.'

Their voices grew louder and louder, until the messenger raised his hand and silence fell. 'The king has heard,' he said, and then he turned and left.

A long time passed, and they thought the king had forgotten them. Early one morning, the deer saw the wolf trotting past the place where she was feeding. She got ready to spring away, but the wolf took no notice of her. A while later, the little girl went by, followed by the horse.

'Where are you going?' called the deer.

'The king has sent us a gift,' replied the horse. 'It may be gold. Come and see.'

The deer left the river's edge and followed the horse along the track through the wood, and across the fields, until they came to the hillside where they had first met with the king's messenger.

There stood a simple, stone hut and outside a small crowd had gathered. The wolf was looking in at the window.

'What is it? What can you see?' asked the deer, forgetting to be afraid.

'It's a baby,' growled the wolf, softly.

'A what?'

'A baby.'

'He won't make the rivers clean,' said the deer.

'He won't free my brothers,' said the wolf.

'He won't stop men fighting,' said the horse.

'He's not rich enough to buy me shoes,' said the little girl, looking at the bare walls.

'Come inside!' called a voice, and they moved forward through the doorway. The king's messenger was standing in the light coming from the window. The farmer was kneeling in the shadows, close to the baby.

'Do you know who this is?' asked the farmer, his eyes wide with wonder.

'No,' they replied.

'This is the king's son. His own son. He's given him to us.'

'Oh,' they said.

They gathered around and looked at the sleeping baby. He was so small, so needy, so new.

'What can he do?' asked the little girl.

The king's messenger raised his hands, and the light streamed from his fingers. 'He will walk where you walk,' he said. 'He will make war on the darkness, and lead you into light. He will make war on death itself, and lead you into life.'

And as they looked at the baby's face, they felt hope begin to stir in their hearts. Their hope grew and made them stronger, and it was as if all around them the air was filled with singing.

We are people of flesh and blood. That is why Jesus became one of us. HEBREWS 2:14

BIBLE REFERENCES

Isaiah 11:1–9; Luke 2:8–20; Hebrews 2:5–18; Revelation 21:1–4

SERMON POINTERS

* **Isaiah 11:1–9:** Why does Isaiah emphasize the effect on the animal kingdom? How much promised here has been accomplished and what is still for the future?
* **Luke 2:8–20:** Why was this news announced to shepherds? What does it tell us about the gospel? In what ways did the shepherds respond?
* **Hebrews 2:5–18:** Why was it essential for Jesus to undergo the same experience as us? What is the outcome for us? How and in what ways are we made holy?
* **Revelation 21:1–4:** How should we view this earth if it is only temporary? Do we see continuity between the present world and the future heaven and earth? How does this affect our life and actions?

QUESTIONS FOR YOUNGER LISTENERS

* What problems did everyone in the story face?
* Can you see the same problems in our world today?
* What did the king do about it?
* Do you think God has done something about it?
* What difference has Jesus made to the world?

VISUAL AIDS AND ACTIONS

* A nativity scene

Gather the children around the scene and tell them the story.

THE LOST DUCKLING

Once there was a duckling who was so busy eating weeds that he didn't notice he'd wandered into a rabbit hole. He'd been told to stay close to his brothers and sisters, but he was too hungry and the weeds were too delicious. Before he knew it, he was in a maze of dark tunnels leading him further and further from the pond.

The first person he saw was a beetle, passing with her family. 'You shouldn't be here,' she snapped. 'Ducks underground! Disgraceful!'

The duckling hurried on, and a worm slithered across the pathway.

'Can you tell me the way to the pond?' asked the duck.

'You're miles away,' said the worm, and disappeared into the tunnel wall.

The duckling wondered what to do. In the darkness he nearly bumped into a mole.

'I'm lost,' he begged. 'Please tell me the way to the pond.'

'Hopeless!' said the mole. 'You'll never find it! Move on, you're blocking the path.'

Soon the duckling came to a junction with tunnels going in all directions. Sitting in one of the tunnels was a huge spider. Its web was filled with shadowy shapes, all very still.

'I'm looking for the pond,' said the duckling nervously.

'Stay here with me,' said the spider. 'We can be friends.' And she stood up and moved forward. The duckling turned and ran back down the tunnel, very frightened.

'What am I going to do?' he whimpered. 'No one will help me.'

He skidded to a stop as the beetle family came round the corner. 'Still here?' said the beetle.

'I'm lost,' replied the duckling.

The beetle tossed her head. 'It's your own fault,' she said, and walked on, tut-tutting to herself.

At this the duckling began to get angry. He'd never been angry before and it was a bit like being very hot. He stamped and shook his feathers, and hissed, and then he shot very fast back the way he'd come, past the spider and down one of the tunnels.

'Whoa, careful!' cried a young rabbit. 'You nearly squashed me. Are you lost?'

'What do you care?' hissed the duckling. 'You're all the same!'

'You are lost. If it would help, I could dig you a new tunnel. Upwards, to the outside.'

The duckling stopped being angry and felt very relieved. 'Thank you,' he said.

'Come on, then,' said the rabbit. 'Follow me.'

So the rabbit scratched and kicked the earth till suddenly the tunnel was flooded with daylight. The duckling scrambled out into the sunshine, and there—some distance away—he could see the shining surface of the pond.

'No one else would help me,' he told the rabbit.

The rabbit laughed. 'Most of them don't know what a pond is,' he said. 'And the rest are too fond of telling other people they're in the wrong. Take no notice of them.'

So the duckling set off to join his brothers and sisters on the pond—and in the future he was very careful about rabbit holes.

God did not send his Son into the world to condemn its people. He sent him to save them! JOHN 3:17

BIBLE REFERENCES

Job 19:1–22; Matthew 7:1–5; John 3:16–18; Romans 2:1–4

SERMON POINTERS

✶ **Job 19:1–22:** What is Job's complaint against his friends? Do we fall into the same error as they did? Is there a way we can offer help rather than condemnation?

✶ **Matthew 7:1–5:** How can we take the log out of our own eye? How might we then be better able to help each other?

✶ **John 3:16–18:** How is God's love demonstrated in these verses? What is the link between faith and eternal life? What leads to condemnation?

✶ **Romans 2:1–4:** Is it true that we often criticize others for faults that we ourselves possess? How can we learn to reflect God's goodness and patience?

QUESTIONS FOR YOUNGER LISTENERS

✶ Why did the duckling go into the rabbit hole?
✶ What help did the duckling need?
✶ How did everyone (except the rabbit) treat him?
✶ How did the rabbit treat him and how did he help him?
✶ How did Jesus treat other people and help them?

VISUAL AIDS AND ACTIONS

✶ A toy or other object

Hide the toy, and then tell the children if they are 'hot' or 'cold' as they move around looking for it.

BEETLE

Mrs Henry was an old lady who lived in an old house with an old garden. It used to belong to her grandparents, and she had often stayed there as a little girl. Someone helped her look after the house, and someone helped her look after the garden. The gardener was called Beetle, and he was very old too. Mrs Henry had known him since he was just a boy and lived in the village.

Mrs Henry told Beetle that her three grandchildren, Stanley, Lloyd and Bella, were coming to stay. Stanley and Lloyd were brothers, and Bella was their cousin.

To begin with, the three children got on very well. This was because they found a common enemy in Beetle. Beetle didn't like them and they didn't like him.

'Whoever heard of anyone called Beetle?' said Stanley. 'He's just a big insect.'

'With a shiny head,' giggled Bella.

'And six legs,' cried Lloyd, and they all collapsed laughing. If ever they found a beetle, they'd put it in the pocket of his jacket hanging in the greenhouse.

'Why can't you go and watch television?' grumbled Beetle. 'Or play those computer games?'

After a while, Lloyd and Stanley found it more fun to tease Bella. They began to make the noise of a bell whenever she came near.

'Ding-dong!' Stanley would say. 'Dinner time!'

'Leave me alone!' cried Bella, and ran into the garden. Beetle had been clearing out the old fishpond, and Bella slipped on the slimy weeds on the grass and fell in.

'Ding-dong bell! Bella's in the well!' sang Lloyd.

Stanley and Lloyd disappeared as Beetle came into view. Bella climbed out of the pond and ran over to the greenhouse. She sat on the steps with her chin on her knees, trying not to cry. 'I hate my name,' she said. 'I hate it.'

'Better than Beetle, isn't it?' asked Beetle.

'No.'

'Well, now, let me tell you something,' said Beetle. 'I've never told anyone this. When I was a baby, my mother thought I was beautiful. So she'd call me her beautiful boy. I couldn't say "beautiful"; I could only say "beetle". It sort of stuck.'

Bella looked up at him with eyes wide open. She couldn't imagine anyone thinking he was beautiful.

'And do you know, that's what Bella means. It doesn't mean bell at all, it means beautiful. You see? We've got the same name in a way.'

Bella wasn't sure if she was pleased about this or not.

'So when anybody teases you, you remember that. It's who you really are that matters, not what people call you. Now, come and help me put the water back in that fishpond. And then you can put the fish in.'

It wasn't long before Stanley and Lloyd realized that Bella was having more fun than they were.

'Beetle's told me all about the fish,' she said, as they stood looking into the pond. That one is called Emperor. He was nearly eaten by a heron. Goldfish can live for nearly forty years. Emperor is about thirty.'

'Thirty!' Lloyd stared in astonishment.

'Beetle also told me,' said Bella, 'that, in their natural state, goldfish are green.'

'Green?' said Stanley. 'Why do we call them goldfish, then?'

'Names aren't always true,' said Bella. 'It's who you really are that matters, not what people call you.'

Anyone who belongs to Christ is a new person.
2 CORINTHIANS 5:17

BIBLE REFERENCES

Genesis 2:18–20; Matthew 1:18–25; Matthew 11:18–19;
2 Corinthians 5:16–18

SERMON POINTERS

* **Genesis 2:18–20**: What is the significance of naming the animals? Does this imply that they are precious? What role is Adam given?
* **Matthew 1:18–25**: Why did it matter what Jesus was called? How did he fulfil the name 'Immanuel'? What other names do we call Jesus?
* **Matthew 11:18–19**: The Pharisees called Jesus 'a friend of sinners'. Why was this meant to be a criticism? Why is it also a sign of grace? What was Jesus' response?
* **2 Corinthians 5:16–18**: How was Jesus judged by what he seemed to be? Do we see beyond appearances with people? Are we prepared to let them 'begin again' as Jesus does?

QUESTIONS FOR YOUNGER LISTENERS

* How were the children unkind to Beetle, and the boys to Bella?
* What did Beetle say was more important than the names people call you?
* What does the name 'Jesus' mean?
* Why is the name of Jesus special?

VISUAL AIDS AND ACTIONS

* A book of names and their meanings

Ask the children what names they have given their pets and toys.

❖

MELISSA THE SNAKE

No one wanted to go near Melissa the snake. It wasn't because she was dangerous but because she said very cruel things. They didn't always sound cruel, but they left you feeling uncomfortable and not quite good enough.

'Young rabbits have such energy,' she said to their mother. 'No wonder you look so faded.'

'Such a good thing you have those bushy tails,' she told a group of squirrels. 'Without them, people might think you were rats.'

'I love bright colours, don't you?' she said to the black-and-white badger.

Then one day she told one of the baby rabbits that he looked fat enough for a fox's dinner. The rabbits decided they had had enough. They got together and thought of a plan.

That night, when Melissa was asleep, they crept forward and tied something to her tail. Melissa was a very long snake, and she liked to sleep coiled round and round a tree trunk. In the morning she woke up to see a strange animal looking at her. It had big yellow eyes, jagged teeth and a round red nose.

'Dear me,' said Melissa. 'You did give me a surprise. I'm afraid there isn't room for you in this part of the world. Not unless you're very special.'

The face dropped a little, and then looked away.

'You have to admit,' smiled Melissa, 'you're not much to look at, are you?'

One of the rabbits came forward. 'Have you made a new friend, Melissa?' he asked.

'We've never met before,' said Melissa haughtily. 'This person is not staying. She finds there are too many rabbits around here.'

Melissa unwound herself from the tree and slid off through the grass. She felt a tug on her tail, and when she looked back the other creature was following her. 'Do leave me alone,' she said. 'It is quite sad the way you're hanging on to me.' But for the whole day Melissa was followed wherever she went. She grew more and more angry, and spoke more and more rudely. 'GO AWAY!' she hissed. 'You are beastly, ugly and STUPID!'

In the evening, Melissa slid down to the pond for a drink. 'Hey, Melissa,' said a heron, perched on one long leg. 'What have you got tied to your tail?'

Then Melissa saw how she'd been tricked. The other creature was just bits of coloured ribbon and paper tied to her tail by the rabbits. She realized that it was herself she'd been horrid to all day, and it wasn't a nice feeling. For the first time in her life, she was speechless. She bit all the ribbon and paper off her tail, and spat them out on to the grass.

'Why did they do it?' she asked the badger who was watching her.

The badger told her. 'Your words can be very unkind sometimes. They wanted *you* to feel how you make them feel.'

Melissa knew he was right. She slipped home and hid for days without speaking to anyone.

'It's my birthday!' called a voice. It was one of the squirrels standing on a branch above her head.

'Happy birthday,' said Melissa quietly.

'You'll come to my party, won't you?'

Melissa was about to say something rude when she stopped herself. 'Yes, I'd like to,' she said.

'You mean it?' asked the squirrel, head on one side.

'Yes,' said Melissa. 'I really mean it.' And she did.

'Your words show what is in your hearts.' MATTHEW 12:34

BIBLE REFERENCES

Proverbs 22:10–11; Matthew 12:33–37; Colossians 4:5–6; James 3:1–18

SERMON POINTERS

* **Proverbs 22:10–11:** What is sincere speech? Is it always kind and polite? Why are insults unacceptable?
* **Matthew 12:33–37:** Do these verses make us uncomfortable? Do we believe we will be accountable for our words? What do we make of Jesus calling the Pharisees 'evil snakes'?
* **Colossians 4:5–6:** How do we speak to those who are not believers? What qualities should our words have? Why?
* **James 3:1–18:** What does James see as the causes and dangers of evil speech? What does he see as the solution? How can we remedy our own speech?

QUESTIONS FOR YOUNGER LISTENERS

* Why did no one like going near Melissa?
* Why did she say such cruel things?
* How did she feel when she found she'd been tricked?
* What did she learn from it?
* How does God want us to speak to each other?

VISUAL AIDS AND ACTIONS

* Paper
* Crayons
* Scissors

Ask the children to draw and colour an animal face and cut it out. You can use one of them in the story.

❖

DRAGON'S GOLD

Once there were two dragons, Dragon Sun and Dragon Stone. They lived in the mountains surrounding a great town, and were so old that they had been there before any human trod the earth.

They were much loved by the townspeople, who believed that the dragons would protect them in times of danger. In fact, it was the other way round. Once, a party of knights on horseback had come to fight the dragons and kill them—but the people in the town had driven them away. The townspeople were led by their own knight, Sir Floren, who was known ever afterwards as the dragons' best friend.

Everyone knows that dragons like to store gold. That is why the knights were coming to kill them, because they'd heard that the dragons were very rich—especially Dragon Sun. He was so rich, it was said that the gold glinted off his scales and glowed in his eyes, and when he looked at you, you could be quite dazzled.

There came a time when the town was in great trouble. The crops had failed due to bad weather, and many people were in distress. Sir Floren climbed up to the caves and called to the dragons. 'Dragon Sun, Dragon Stone, our town is in trouble. Please spare us some gold, or the poor will starve.'

Dragon Stone called out from his cave, 'No one can eat gold.'

'You are right,' replied Floren. 'But a party of us are going to cross the mountains in search of food. We need the gold to buy grain.'

Dragon Stone grumbled softly. 'Ask Dragon Sun,' he said. 'He's rich enough not to notice the loss of a few coins.'

'Of course,' said Dragon Sun. 'I would be glad to help. Your town has been so good to us.' And out of his cave rolled a large sack of gold.

'Thank you!' cried Floren. 'Here, let me leave you my sword in return. It is all I have to give you.' And he laid his long, silver sword in the mouth of the cave.

After that, other people began climbing the mountains to ask the dragons for gold. Dragon Stone kept telling them that he had very little, and that Dragon Sun was the rich one. Dragon Sun would talk to them about their lives, their work and their families, and they never left without a few coins in their pockets. Some people felt that Dragon Sun was so rich he could have done more, and they grumbled at the little he gave. Others were grateful and left him gifts—a child's wooden cradle, a walking-stick, a piece of embroidered cloth.

At last, Floren and his party returned with donkeys laden with grain, and the people of the town gathered round, knowing that their hunger was at an end.

There came a day when the two dragons, who were very old, closed their eyes for the last time and died. The townspeople were very sad, and went up to the caves to say goodbye. To their astonishment, in the dark shadows of Dragon Stone's cave they found a huge pile of gold and precious jewels—more wealth than they had ever imagined. In Dragon Sun's cave, they found only a handful of coins and the gifts that the townspeople had brought. Laid across them was the silver sword that had belonged to Floren.

'We thought Dragon Sun was rich!' they said in surprise. Floren lifted his sword from the earth and ran it back into its scabbard.

'There are different ways of being rich,' he said. 'Dragon Sun was rich at heart, and that's why he'll be remembered.'

And taking one last look around him, he left the cave and climbed back down the mountain.

> **They were glad to give generously.** 2 CORINTHIANS 8:2

BIBLE REFERENCES

Ruth 2:1–23; Luke 21:1–4; 2 Corinthians 8:1–12;
1 Timothy 6:17–19

SERMON POINTERS

* **Ruth 2:1–23**: How had Ruth shown herself generous, even though she was poor? How did Boaz show himself generous, even though he was rich?
* **Luke 21:1–4**: Do we give only as much as we can easily spare? What was the woman's attitude in these verses?
* **2 Corinthians 8:1–12**: How does giving relate to the kindness of God in this passage? What was the condition of the Macedonian church? Do we think that only the rich should give?
* **1 Timothy 6:17–19**: What is the warning here for rich believers? What are they asked to do? How will it benefit them?

QUESTIONS FOR YOUNGER LISTENERS

* In what ways were the two dragons different from each other?
* Which do you think had most money?
* Why was Dragon Sun willing to help the townspeople?
* What are the ways we can give to other people?
* How can we give to God?

VISUAL AIDS AND ACTIONS

* Purse
* Cheque book
* Piggy bank
* Cash box
* Jewel case

Talk about the places where we store our treasure.

KITE FLYING

It was wedged in its box, covered in plastic cellophane, a roll of peacock blue cloth coiled around with long scarlet ribbons.

'What is it?' asked Meena. 'Is it a firework?'

'It's a kite,' said Sanjeev. He drew out the cloth and unwrapped it. Several long sticks fell out in a bundle on to the table.

'Are there any instructions?' asked their mother. She picked up a piece of printed paper. 'Goodness. This looks complicated.'

'I can do it,' said Sanjeev. 'Hang on, there's a note from Dad. "Happy birthday and happy flying."' Sanjeev's face shone with excitement.

After school, Sanjeev's friend Jake came round for tea. Sanjeev showed him the kite.

'How high can it fly?' asked Jake.

'As high as the sky,' said Sanjeev.

'Aren't you going to unwrap it?' asked Meena. 'It's not doing much in its box.'

''Course I am,' said Sanjeev. He began slotting the sticks into the blue cloth while Jake held the sheet of instructions. It took longer than he thought to thread the strings in the right way, and undo all the knots that kept appearing in the wrong places.

'That's it,' he said at last.

'Cool!' cried Jake.

'It's not flying,' said Meena.

'You have to make it fly,' Sanjeev told her. 'Come on.'

There was a path at the bottom of their garden that led to some open land. The three of them carried the kite carefully down the path, Meena holding the ends of the red ribbons. They laid it down on the ground, and Sanjeev took hold of the strings. He wasn't sure what to do next.

'You have to run,' Jake told him. Sanjeev ran, and the kite bounced along the ground a little, but nothing more.

'Faster!' cried Meena. Sanjeev ran and ran across the grass, as fast as he could. He looked back, and the kite was flapping in the air behind him like some wounded bird.

When he stopped, it fell to the ground and lay still.

'It's not much good,' said Jake. 'I've seen better kites than that.'

Sanjeev felt ashamed. He wondered why his dad had sent him a kite that didn't fly. The next day, after school, he decided to try again, this time on his own. There was a strong breeze blowing, and Sanjeev had trouble carrying the kite across the open ground. He placed it flat and walked away holding the strings, then began to pull. Immediately, the kite lifted into the air, higher and higher, tugging at his arms so that he struggled to hold on. 'It's the wind, the wind!' cried Sanjeev. 'That's what makes it fly!'

The kite dipped suddenly and hurtled to one side, and then down towards the ground. Sanjeev pulled hard on one of the strings, and the kite circled up again till it was bobbing high above his head. The scarlet ribbons flew beneath it, swirling and weaving patterns in the air.

Gradually Sanjeev learnt to control the kite, to give the strings just the right tug at the right time, and to make it dance against the sky. And all the while, the wind blew at his back and lifted his arms so that he felt as if he, too, were flying.

> **This is God's gift to you, and not anything you have done on your own.** EPHESIANS 2:8

BIBLE REFERENCES

Ezekiel 37:1–14; Mark 2:1–12; Ephesians 2:1–10;
2 Thessalonians 1:11–12

SERMON POINTERS

★ **Ezekiel 37:1–14**: What did God ask the bones to do? What did he ask the people of Israel to do? What did God promise them?

★ **Mark 2:1–12**: What did the crippled man have to do to be healed and forgiven? What part did faith play in this story?

★ **Ephesians 2:1–10**: What is required of us in these verses? How can we live the life God plans for us?

★ **2 Thessalonians 1:11–12**: What do we need along with our good intentions? How can we be sure of God's help? Do we pray for each other as Paul prayed?

QUESTIONS FOR YOUNGER LISTENERS

★ What made the kite fly?
★ What did Sanjeev have to do?
★ How does God help us to live the Christian life?
★ What do we have to do to live the Christian life?

VISUAL AIDS AND ACTIONS

★ A kite

Ask who can fly a kite. Talk about what it can do.

THE UNGRATEFUL TORTOISE

Once there was a tortoise who was saved from a horrible death by an elephant. A branch had fallen on her, pinning her down and slowly squashing her. The elephant saw the tortoise in difficulties and lifted off the heavy branch. The tortoise gasped for breath and blinked her eyes.

'I suppose you dropped that branch on purpose,' she snapped.

'I didn't drop it,' said the elephant.

'Well, I dare say you shook the ground so much, you made it fall.' The tortoise began crawling away. She was limping badly.

'Can I help at all?' asked the elephant. 'Can I carry you somewhere?'

The tortoise came to a stop. 'I'm heading for the river. It'll take me a week. I don't expect I'll ever make it with this leg.'

The elephant curled his trunk round the tortoise and lifted her on to his head.

'And how am I meant to stay on?' she cried. 'It hasn't occurred to you that I could fall off and be killed!'

'Hold on to my ears,' said the elephant. They travelled fast through the forest, until the tortoise complained that she felt seasick and the elephant slowed down. They reached the river and the elephant placed her carefully on the ground.

'We're on the south side,' grumbled the tortoise. 'I was going to go further upriver to the bridge and cross over. But it's too late now.'

'I can swim,' said the elephant. 'Sit on my head again and I'll take you across.'

'What about crocodiles? Of course they won't attack you, but have you thought how dangerous it could be for me?'

'Don't worry,' said the elephant kindly. 'I'll keep them away.'

The elephant waded into the water and began swimming. The tortoise was splashed by the waves and complained the whole journey.

'Here we are.' The elephant reached the opposite side and lowered his head. 'Climb on to the bank, and we'll say goodbye. I'm going back to the forest.'

'That's fine for you,' said the tortoise. 'I don't suppose you care what happens to me.'

The tortoise walked under a bush and began munching the leaves. She felt cross and her leg hurt. She also felt very lonely. At first she was angry with the elephant for leaving her. She carried on being angry till she had stripped the bush of nearly all its leaves. She moved on to the next one, and then she began to think about the way she'd behaved. By the time she got to the third bush she had reached a decision.

It took her a week to walk to the bridge, and another week to find the elephant.

'I've come to say sorry,' she said. 'You were so kind to me and all I did was complain.'

'Perhaps your leg was hurting,' said the elephant.

'No. It wasn't that. I just didn't want to say "thank you". I was so angry about the branch and I wanted to blame you. I'm not a very nice tortoise.'

'I think you are,' said the elephant. 'Or you wouldn't have come back.'

The tortoise went pink inside her shell. 'Thank you,' she said. 'Thank you.'

And she felt as if the branch had been lifted off her all over again.

> **Whatever happens, keep thanking God because of Jesus Christ.** 1 THESSALONIANS 5:18

BIBLE REFERENCES

1 Chronicles 16:7–13; Luke 17:11–19; Philippians 4:4–7;
1 Thessalonians 5:15–18

SERMON POINTERS

* **1 Chronicles 16:7–13**: David was a great giver of thanks to God. Are we like that, or do we give thanks grudgingly?
* **Luke 17:11–19**: What can we learn about the Samaritan in this story? Do we thank God for our blessings or only dwell on the problems?
* **Philippians 4:4–7**: Is this the secret of happiness? What qualities do we see in happy people? Does God's peace control our thinking and feeling?
* **1 Thessalonians 5:15–18**: What is our chief reason to thank God? Can we really be expected to thank God 'whatever happens'? If so, why?

QUESTIONS FOR YOUNGER LISTENERS

* What kind of person was the elephant?
* What do you think of the tortoise?
* Do you think the tortoise learned to behave differently?
* Are we good at saying 'thank you'?
* What reasons do we have to say 'thank you' to God?

VISUAL AIDS AND ACTIONS

* 'Thank you' cards

Ask the children to suggest a variety of messages—'thank you for my present', 'thank you for your prayers' and so on.

'READY ABOUT'

'It's all right for you,' said Ben. 'Your dad owns the boatyard. You can go out in boats any time you want.'

'Come on, Josh,' said Lucy. 'Take us out in a boat.'

Josh felt nervous. He knew what his dad would say if he took a boat out, but he didn't want to let his friends down.

'Just round the harbour,' pleaded Deepak.

Josh looked at the boats. There was a yacht moored near the end of the jetty, which his dad had been working on.

'OK,' he agreed. 'Not for long, though.'

Josh helped his friends on board and then undid the mooring rope. They motored around the harbour for a while, till the others got bored.

'Take us out to sea!' said Ben.

'Can't you go faster?' cried Deepak.

There was a good breeze blowing across the entrance to the harbour, and Josh decided to put up the sails. 'This'll be fast,' he thought. He began to enjoy himself. He'd often been out sailing with his dad, and on his own in the harbour in a dinghy.

But his friends had no idea what to do. Lucy nearly fell overboard when Deepak pushed past her, and Ben let go of the ropes so that the main sail swung out over the side. Immediately the wind blew the boat round and tipped it at an angle. There was a crash or two from the cabin, and Josh's friends gripped tight and yelled.

'Josh!' called a sharp voice from the cabin.

'Dad!' cried Josh.

'Get those lifejackets on!'

Josh obeyed his father, handing round the lifejackets he'd taken from the lockers. His friends stared as Josh's dad climbed out into the cockpit and winched in the ropes quickly to get the sail under control.

'Right, we're going to turn round,' he said, one hand on the rudder. 'Listen hard. That beam with the sail on is going to cross over the cockpit, and it'll knock down anyone who's standing up. When I call "gybe", you need to mind your heads. Here goes! Ready about! Heads down, everyone; watch the boom. Gybe!'

Josh pulled in the ropes as the boom passed over their heads. The boat swung round and began to move back towards the harbour mouth.

As they tied up next to the jetty, Josh's dad looked at his friends sternly. 'Now I've got a few things to say to my son,' he said. He waited till the three of them had walked away over the planks. Then he turned to Josh. Josh felt his hands go sweaty.

'I can't accuse you of stealing, because you're my son. But I can tell you this, you should know better.'

'Yes, Dad,' said Josh.

'You should know better, because you're lucky. You're lucky I taught you how to sail. You're lucky you've had the chance to go on boats all your life. But if you or any of your friends had drowned, how lucky would you have been then?'

'Yes, Dad,' said Josh.

'Most of all, you're lucky I was still on board.'

'Yes, Dad,' said Josh. 'I know.'

'Then next time,' said his dad, 'you ask me. And we'll see how good your friends are in a dinghy before they take to sea.'

'Yes, Dad,' said Josh. And then, as his father put an arm round his shoulders, he added, 'Thanks.'

> **Don't let sin keep ruling your lives.** ROMANS 6:14

BIBLE REFERENCES

2 Samuel 12:1–10; Matthew 3:7–10; Romans 6:1–23; Jude 3–4

SERMON POINTERS

★ **2 Samuel 12:1–10**: How did David abuse his privilege? How can we avoid abusing the privileges God has given us as Christians?

★ **Matthew 3:7–10**: What attitude does John the Baptist condemn? What does he tell the Pharisees to do? Are we in danger of the same attitude?

★ **Romans 6:1–23**: Does God's kindness to us free us from restraint? Or does it give different grounds for restraint? What is Paul's argument here, and why is it necessary?

★ **Jude 3–4**: What heresy is Jude writing about? Do we reflect the same complacency? What does Jude claim our attitude to Christ should be?

QUESTIONS FOR YOUNGER LISTENERS

★ Was Josh free to go out on his father's boat?
★ Why did he do so with his friends?
★ What did his father say to him afterwards?
★ Does God love us even when we do wrong?
★ Does that mean that we can do what we like?

VISUAL AIDS AND ACTIONS

★ A model of a boat or a buoyancy aid

Ask the children what boats they have been on, and one thing they remember about the experience.

BROTHER JONAS

Brother Jonas was a very good person. He was kind and gentle and caring towards everyone. People found him easy to talk to. He never lost his temper, he never quarrelled with anyone, and he never said rude words or slammed doors. He was always willing to help.

But he did make other people cross. It was amazing how even the mildest of monks would lose their temper and say rude words when he was around. The reason was that Brother Jonas was very clumsy. Whatever he touched, he broke. Every time he washed up after a meal, something would get dropped or chipped. If he did the gardening, his big feet would crush as many flowers as he planted. Even climbing the stairs or walking along the corridors, he would bump into things and scratch them.

Once he helped to wash the monastery windows, but he was never asked again.

The monastery made wooden bowls and carved ornaments and crosses, which they sold to visitors. Brother Jonas helped to make them. Brother Mark, the monk in charge of the workshop, set him to sanding and polishing the newly carved wood, thinking that he could do little damage with a piece of sandpaper.

Jonas was very helpful. But then, another monk nearly lost a finger because Jonas knocked into him as he was doing some fine chisel work. After this, Brother Mark went to see the abbot, and the abbot sent for Brother Jonas.

Brother Jonas was a novice monk. He hadn't yet taken his final vows to stay in the monastery, and the abbot told him that it might be a good idea if he never did. 'We can't afford you,' said the abbot. 'You break more than you make.'

Brother Jonas went away with his heart heavier than he had ever known it before. He was on cleaning duty, and as he polished the banisters up the stairway, for the first time he found it hard to take any joy in watching the dark wood grow shiny and bright.

The abbot, meanwhile, knelt to say his prayers. He prayed for all the monks in his monastery. He even said a prayer for Brother Jonas. He said a prayer for the visitors each Sunday, and those staying in the visitors' house. And then he stopped, because for some reason he was sure God was not listening. The abbot waited, and thought, and meditated, and prayed. But there was nothing. Something was wrong. The next day was the same, and the day after that. Then, one evening as it grew late, the abbot went into the chapel and knelt at the altar.

'Father God,' he prayed, 'tell me why you seem so distant from me.'

Out of the shadows the words floated into his head. 'I can't afford you. You break more than you make.'

The abbot bent his head in shame. He called Brother Jonas to him. 'Brother,' he said, 'I was wrong to speak to you as I did. You are here among us as a gift of God. You show us how God looks on us and loves us. You are welcome.'

Brother Jonas smiled broadly and tripped over his big feet as he left the room. But inside he was dancing.

> **Forgive anyone who does you wrong, just as Christ has forgiven you.** COLOSSIANS 3:13

BIBLE REFERENCES

Micah 6:6–8; Mark 11:25–26; Luke 11:1–4; Colossians 3:12–14

SERMON POINTERS

✶ **Micah 6:6–8:** What do we learn about true worship from these verses? How does this apply to our church services and our church life?

* **Mark 11:25–26:** Is Jesus saying that God's forgiveness begins with us being willing to forgive? Or is he expressing how they are interconnected?
* **Luke 11:1–4:** Jesus' teaching on prayer endorses the link between forgiving and being forgiven. Do we emphasize this enough in our church prayers?
* **Colossians 3:12–14:** What does Paul give as the basis of our forgiveness and acceptance of others?

QUESTIONS FOR YOUNGER LISTENERS

* Why did the abbot want to get rid of Brother Jonas?
* What happened when he tried to pray?
* How did God want the abbot to treat Brother Jonas?
* How does God want us to treat each other?

VISUAL AIDS AND ACTIONS

* A pile of toy bricks on a table

These, or other objects, could be 'accidentally' knocked over before the talk, or as a sound effect during it.

THE REVENGE VIRUS

Barney Fisher was brilliant at computers—but he wasn't brilliant at talking to people.

So when his best friend at school, Joe, upset him, Barney sent him an e-mail. It took him a month to write. The reason it took him so long was that the e-mail was a virus. He called it 'The Revenge Virus'.

It was meant to go to everyone on Joe's address list, and leave the message 'I hate you' all over the screen. Barney felt good as he pressed the 'Send' button. He thought of all Joe's friends and family being upset and angry, thinking the message came from Joe.

A few days later, Barney opened an e-mail from someone he knew in Australia. It was a girl, and she was very special to Barney. The message read, 'I hate you too.'

Barney was horrified. What did she mean? Then other e-mails began to come, with the same kind of message. He worked out what had happened. The Revenge Virus had sent itself to everyone on his address list as well, and also to their address lists. People he'd never heard of began sending him angry messages. A wave of hate was spreading from friend to friend across the whole world, and it was all his fault. All because he'd wanted to pay someone back for hurting him.

'I don't know how to stop it,' he thought. 'What shall I do?' He felt he was evil, as if *he* had the Revenge Virus himself. He wanted to cry, and run and hide. He couldn't face going to classes.

In the end, Barney went to see Joe. He didn't e-mail him, or phone him, or text him. He went to see him. It took all his courage. Joe listened as Barney told him what he had done. Joe was very angry.

'Why, Barney?' he said. 'Why did you do that to me?'

Barney explained. 'Your uncle runs a computer firm. I wanted to work for him after college. But then you told him I couldn't be trusted.'

Joe stared at him. 'Where did you get that idea?'

'Your sister. She heard you.'

Joe looked annoyed. 'She heard wrong. I never said that. I said you're always coming up with new ideas, and no one can guess what you'll do next. I thought I was doing you a favour.'

Barney felt terrible. 'I'm sorry,' he said. 'I got it all wrong. What shall I do about the virus?'

Joe thought for a minute. 'I'll ask my uncle,' he said.

A week later, Barney received an e-mail from Joe. It read 'Virus sorted.'

Barney felt a great weight lift from his heart. He wrote to everyone on his mailing list, saying, 'I'm very sorry. Please forgive me. Barney.'

Then Barney received a letter from Joe's uncle. 'Come and talk to me,' he wrote. 'We need people with new ideas.'

Barney sent a text message to Joe. 'You're a good friend, Joe,' he said. 'Thanks.'

Don't try to take revenge. LEVITICUS 19:18

BIBLE REFERENCES

Leviticus 19:17–18; Luke 23:32–34; Romans 12:14–21; 2 Corinthians 2:5–11

SERMON POINTERS

✷ **Leviticus 19:17–18:** What is the difference between revenge and correction? What part does love play?

✷ **Luke 23:32–34:** Whom is Jesus asking his father to forgive? What do these words reveal about Jesus? Are we capable of the same attitude?

★ **Romans 12:14–21:** Who curses us, and do we bless them? Why should we leave revenge to God? How can good defeat evil?

★ **2 Corinthians 2:5–11:** Do we know, as a church community, how to forgive and restore each other? Why does Paul see this as so important?

QUESTIONS FOR YOUNGER LISTENERS

★ What made Barney send 'The Revenge Virus'? What did he feel like inside?

★ Is there a better way he could have acted towards Joe?

★ How did Barney feel when he realized the virus had spread?

★ Did Jesus take revenge on people? What did he say on the cross?

VISUAL AIDS AND ACTIONS

★ Mobile phone
★ Paper in a bottle
★ A book
★ A letter

Ask the children to list all the different ways to send messages.

❖

THE SORRY SQUIRRELS

'Keep that noise down!' shouted the old oak tree.

'Sorry!' called the squirrels. They raced to the ground and began digging. Their parents had buried some acorns nearby, and they were always hoping to find them.

Two of the squirrels, Sam and Ginger, began quarrelling. Sam got bitten and squealed loudly.

'Stop that fighting!' cried the oak tree.

'Sorry!' called the squirrels. Sam chased Ginger back up the tree and the rest followed, chirping and laughing.

'I won't have you running about my branches like hooligans!' The oak tree shook his leaves in fury. 'It's the same every day. Every day! What's the matter with you?'

'Sorry!' said the squirrels. They sat very still for a moment, clinging to the tree, and then Ginger was off again while they all followed. Up he went, as high as he could, then he ran down the other side, along a branch and leapt over to a lime tree.

The next day, as the sun rose, the squirrels bounded from tree to tree all the way from the road to the river. They reached the oak tree and bounced all over him. He was only just waking up and was not in a good mood. He curled the toes of his roots further into the soil, and leant over towards the river. How nice it would be if he could shake off all the squirrels into the water, and watch them float away.

Suddenly, one of them scratched his bark and bit him. 'Ow!' he yelped.

'Sorry!' said the squirrel. 'I was trying to reach a caterpillar.'

The other squirrels all began looking for caterpillars, and soon the oak tree was being scratched and bitten all over.

'No, no, no!' he cried. 'That's enough! Go away, all of you!' He shook himself violently and the squirrels began scampering down the trunk in alarm. One of them fell, and thumped painfully against the ground.

'You horrible old tree!' shouted Ginger. 'We'll never climb you again!'

'Good!' said the oak tree. 'Next time I'll shake you into the river!'

The squirrels ran away, muttering to themselves. They were very angry. After that they kept away from the oak tree and played in the other trees.

One tree was a willow, its long slender branches trailing down into the water. 'I can swing on those branches right over the river!' boasted Sam.

'Careful!' one of them cried out. 'They look very thin!'

All the squirrels stood around and watched as Sam clung to the swaying branch. But when he tried to leap to another branch, the wind blew it out of his reach and he fell towards the water.

Within seconds he was being carried down the river. 'After him!' shouted Ginger.

From treetop to treetop they leapt, keeping just ahead of him, until they reached the oak tree.

One of the oak tree's branches grew low over the water. Ginger had an idea, and all the squirrels followed him on to the branch. Just as Sam came into sight, the squirrels began bouncing up and down, causing the branch to dip in and out of the water. The oak tree was too shocked to speak.

'Hold on!' cried Ginger as Sam came close. Sam grabbed a bunch of leaves trailing in the water and curled himself round them. The squirrels stopped bouncing, and the branch lifted clear of the river.

'Wow, that was fun!' said Sam. 'Come on, let's go.'

'Stop a minute!' cried the oak tree sternly. 'I have something to say to you all.'

'Sorry!' they said automatically.

'No. *I* want to say that *I'm* sorry—for being so unfriendly. I thought I wanted to be alone and quiet, but I missed you all. I hope you will come back soon.'

The squirrels thought for a minute. 'I suppose we could try to be quieter,' they said.

'And I could show *you*,' said the oak tree, 'where all those acorns are hidden. You'll never find them where you've been looking.'

> **'Let the children come to me! Don't try to stop them.'**
> MARK 10:14

BIBLE REFERENCES

1 Chronicles 22:6–16; Mark 10:13–16; Acts 15:36–41;
Colossians 4:10

SERMON POINTERS

* **1 Chronicles 22:6–16**: How did David respond to God's choice of Solomon to build the temple? What can we learn from this in our attitude to the next generation?
* **Mark 10:13–16**: What are the different attitudes adults have to children in this passage? What might the equivalent be in our churches? What does Jesus teach about children?
* **Acts 15:36–41**: What is the cause of conflict in these verses? Was Paul expecting too much from Mark? What expectations do we have of younger people?
* **Colossians 4:10**: What does this verse tell us about the relationship between Paul and Mark? What can we learn from this conclusion?

QUESTIONS FOR YOUNGER LISTENERS

* Why was the oak tree so upset?
* Did the squirrels mean it when they said 'sorry'?
* Were you surprised when the oak tree said 'sorry'?
* How did the disciples feel about the children who came to see Jesus?
* What did Jesus say to them about children?

VISUAL AIDS AND ACTIONS

✷ Play 'Sleeping squirrels', where the children have to be motionless. Anyone who moves or twitches is out.

THE TWO GIANTS

Once there were two giants who were brothers. Their names were Giant Grub and Giant Grime, and they lived next door to each other. But because they were such good friends, they had broken a hole through the wall and put in a doorway so that they could easily go between the two houses.

'Are you there, Grime?' Grub would call. 'I've been baking biscuits. Would you like some?'

'Bring a barrel,' Grime called back, 'and come and watch the football with me.'

Now, one day, the nearby villagers heard a terrible noise. At first they thought it was thunder or an earthquake or an explosion, but then they realized it was the giants shouting at each other.

'You've been wearing my boots!' shouted Grime. 'They don't fit me any more.'

'That's because they're my boots!' yelled Grub. 'Yours are worn out.'

'They're mine!'

'No, they're not, they're mine!'

Giants are very fussy about their boots. They have such big feet that comfortable boots are hard to find—and if their feet aren't comfortable they get very bad-tempered.

Grime and Grub stormed and shouted for the best part of a day. In the evening the villagers heard hammering and banging going on. It went on all night, and nobody was able to sleep.

The brothers had nailed up the doorway between their two homes. They'd used planks of wood, chair legs, floorboards, anything they could get. Each of them had nailed up their own side.

After that, there was quiet. But from time to time the villagers would hear more hammering, because every time the brothers remembered how the other had treated them, they would bang another nail into the doorway.

A year went by, and the giants never spoke to each other. There were the usual sounds from next door, walking about and sneezing, bath water running, doors slamming, and sometimes the television on very loud. But that was all.

Then, one day, Giant Grub noticed how quiet it was. He realized he hadn't heard his brother for days. The thought struck him, 'Is he all right?' But he banged another nail in, to show he didn't care.

Grub left it another day and a half, and then he knew he had to find out. He went next door and pressed his face against the window. There was no one there. But what he did see made him gasp. Over the months, his brother Grime had taken every piece of wood and every nail out of the doorway, and the only thing left blocking the entrance was the wood on Grub's side.

Grub felt his heart would burst. What a selfish, stupid giant he'd been! How ugly to be so angry. And now his brother was missing, and he might never see him again.

Grub went home and wept and wept. While the tears were falling, he tore down the horrible barrier to his brother's house—the layers and layers of wood fixed with hundreds of nails.

Two days later, a postcard fell on to the doormat. Grub read it.

'Having a great time. Weather good. Back next week. Grime.'

His brother had gone on holiday! Grub laughed and cried at the same time. When Grime did come home, he found his own house warm and clean, with fresh baking in the kitchen. And between the two houses was a doorway so big that nothing could ever block it again.

Stop being bitter and angry with others. EPHESIANS 4:31

BIBLE REFERENCES

Micah 7:18–20; Proverbs 15:18; Matthew 5:21–24; Ephesians 4:25–32

SERMON POINTERS

✶ **Micah 7:18–20**: What do we learn here about God's character? Why do some people imagine God as always angry?

✶ **Proverbs 15:18**: What is wrong with losing your temper? Is it different from being angry? How can we be better at settling arguments?

✶ **Matthew 5:21–24**: Why does Jesus link anger and insults with murder? Is this going too far? What is our experience of anger?

✶ **Ephesians 4:25–32**: What are the reasons given for this code of behaviour? Should we learn to control our anger? How?

QUESTIONS FOR YOUNGER LISTENERS

✶ Why do you think Grime took the wood and nails out of his side of the doorway?

✶ Why did Grub do the same?

✶ Do you ever get angry like the two giants in this story? Who with?

✶ What does Jesus teach us about forgiving each other?

VISUAL AIDS AND ACTIONS

✶ Hammer
✶ Nails
✶ A piece of wood

Hammer in some nails for emphasis at appropriate stages in the story.

NEW YEAR'S EVE

'Who's that man, Grandad?' I asked, watching through the window as the stranger turned away from the front door.

'That's Mr Styles, Jenny,' said my grandfather. 'Mr Benjamin Styles.'

'Why didn't you answer the door?' I climbed off the bench and went over to my grandfather's chair.

'I never do. He comes every year. Regular. New Year's Eve. And he goes away again.'

My grandfather was a kind man, but he didn't sound kind then. I wondered what the other man had done to him, but I was too afraid to ask. My parents had gone shopping in town, and had left me there for the day. They'd warned me I had to be good.

I caught sight of a piece of paper on the doormat. 'He's left a note,' I said.

'He always does.' My grandfather took it from me, and stuffed it into his jacket pocket. My eyes grew rounder and I stared at him. He saw my face and said, 'You want to know, don't you? Who he is? You want the story?'

I nodded.

'All right then.' Grandad settled back into his chair and fixed his eyes on a corner of the room. 'It was a long time ago. There were two men, friends since they were lads. Each had a bit of a farm—not much, but a living. One of them had ideas of growing rich, having a bigger farm. So he tried to buy the other one out, made him an offer, but it was refused.'

I knew Grandad had been a farmer when he was young, but had given it up before my mother was born. I hung on to the arm of his chair and listened.

'Now there was a river flowing through both pieces of land. They needed it to water their cattle and anything they were growing. They didn't have piped water, they lived too high in the hills, and it was too remote. So the first young man hit on an idea. On his own land, he dug a channel away from the river, so that most of the water went a different way. Only a small stream was left to run into the other man's land.'

My grandfather paused and took out the stranger's note. He crumpled it in one of his fists, and carried on.

'When the other man found he had no water, he tried to persuade his friend to block up the channel. He tried to do it himself one night. But in the end, he could do nothing. He had to sell his live-stock, and the land was worth very little. That's when the first man bought it up, cheap, and the other one went away. I expect you've guessed. Those two young men were myself and Ben Styles. The rich Mr Benjamin Styles.'

'That's bad!' I said. 'What a bad man! No wonder you don't let him in! Why does he keep coming?'

'He wants to be friends again. But you can't undo what's done, Jenny. You have to live with it.'

'Maybe he's changed,' I said, beginning to feel sorry for Mr Styles.

'People don't change.' My grandfather gave a sigh and tossed the note across the room. He closed his eyes, and after a few moments he was dozing.

I crept across the room and uncurled the note. It read: 'Come on, Jack, it's a new year starting. Another new year. Let's forget the past. I forgive you, Jack. I forgave you long ago for digging that channel. Can't you believe me, and be friends?'

The note was signed 'Ben'.

It had been my grandfather who had stopped the river flowing into Ben's land, and not the other way round. I went over to the window and looked out. There was no sign of anyone. The air was empty and cold, and a few flakes of snow had started to fall.

'If you hear my voice and open the door, I will come in and we will eat together.' REVELATION 3:20

BIBLE REFERENCES

Proverbs 3:11–12; Matthew 27:3–5; Hebrews 3:7–19;
Revelation 3:14–22

SERMON POINTERS

✶ **Proverbs 3:11–12:** How do we respond to God's correction? What form might it take? How does it strengthen our relationship with him?
✶ **Matthew 27:3–5:** What emotions did Judas go through? Why did he act in this way? Was he beyond the reach of God's forgiveness?
✶ **Hebrews 3:7–19:** What is the warning underlying these verses? Where does faith come in? When do we show stubbornness?
✶ **Revelation 3:14–22:** What mistakes have the Laodiceans made? What does Jesus promise them? Are these promises true for us as well?

QUESTIONS FOR YOUNGER LISTENERS

✶ Why did Ben Styles visit Jenny's grandfather every year?
✶ Why didn't her grandfather let him in?
✶ How might Jenny have felt at the end of the story?
✶ Do we ignore God sometimes?
✶ How can we let God into our lives?

VISUAL AIDS AND ACTIONS

✶ A piece of notepaper

Use the notepaper as a visual aid as it appears in the story.

ABEL THE ROBOT

Mr Frank built robots. His best robot was called Abel. Abel was programmed to mow the lawn and make toast and wash the car.

Mr Frank had a son called Jonathan. Jonathan was more difficult to programme. Mr Frank tried very hard, but he admitted he knew nothing about young people.

Mr Frank spent most of his life in his workshop. When he came into the house, he would say, 'Jonathan, have you done your homework yet? Are those your boots in the hall? What about helping to wash up for a change? Are you listening to me?'

But Jonathan never did listen. His father didn't know what to do. At last he decided to try Abel. Mr Frank wrote a new programme and fed in all the data he could on his son.

Abel clicked and buzzed, and lights flashed on the top of his head. Then he set off to find Jonathan. Mr Frank followed, eager to see what would happen.

First, Abel challenged Jonathan to a game of chess. Jonathan refused. 'What's the point?' he said. 'You always win.' But then he added, 'How about football?'

Now Abel had a huge brain, but he couldn't kick a football, because if he lifted up one of his legs too high, he fell over.

'All right,' said Abel. 'You teach me.'

Jonathan couldn't believe it. 'OK, here goes.' He flipped a football up in the air towards the robot. It landed on Abel's head and bounced on to the grass.

'Goal!' cried Abel.

'It's not a goal, idiot!' said Jonathan. He bounced the ball on his knee a couple of times and then caught it on his foot. 'Can you do this?'

Abel stuck a leg out, and put one arm on the ground to support himself. The ball rolled down his leg and fell off. 'No,' he said.

'I'll try you in goal.' Jonathan made a goal mouth with his jersey and a couple of bricks. Then he kicked the ball hard. Abel clanked forward, put both arms straight up in the air, and fell over. There was a pop as the ball burst.

'Game over,' said Jonathan.

'I like football,' said Abel.

Mr Frank had had enough. He took Abel back to the workshop. 'What are you doing?' he said. 'You're as bad as he is. You're just messing about with a football.'

He took Abel's head off to see if any wires were loose. He tried rewriting the programme. In the end he gave up.

'I need a new football, Dad,' said Jonathan that evening. 'Abel squashed it.'

Mr Frank sighed. 'I know. I think I'll dismantle him.'

'What?' Jonathan was horrified. 'He was doing his best, Dad. It's not his fault.'

'I'll make a new robot—one that can play better.'

'No, Dad, he's great the way he is. I like him.'

Mr Frank looked at his son in surprise. He'd never heard Jonathan say he liked anyone. An idea came to him. 'We could go to town tomorrow,' he said. 'You can buy a new football. You can try it out in the park.'

'OK,' Jonathan agreed. 'Abel and I can teach *you* to play.'

Mr Frank felt suddenly nervous. He thought of all the work he had to do. He thought of how hard it was to talk to Jonathan. But then he thought how good it might be just to spend some time with him. 'OK, son,' he said.

Abel didn't smile, because he wasn't made that way, but deep in his head a small wire glowed.

He will lead children and parents to love each other more.
MALACHI 4:6

BIBLE REFERENCES

Malachi 4:5–6; Luke 2:41–52; Ephesians 6:1–4; 2 Timothy 1:1–8

SERMON POINTERS

* **Malachi 4:5–6:** How and why did God intend to bring children and parents together?
* **Luke 2:41–52:** What do we read about the relationship between Jesus and his parents? What was the tension? Do we underestimate God's presence in the lives of young people?
* **Ephesians 6:1–4:** How does this mutual responsibility reflect the verse in Malachi?
* **2 Timothy 1:1–8:** How does Paul show himself to be a good father-figure in his relationship with Timothy? Can we identify such figures in our lives?

QUESTIONS FOR YOUNGER LISTENERS

* What was the problem between Mr Frank and Jonathan?
* How did Mr Frank try to solve it?
* What did Mr Frank learn from Abel?
* What did Jesus teach us about God as our Father?

VISUAL AIDS AND ACTIONS

* A few football-sized softballs

Ask the children to run and kick a ball around, while keeping their two feet together!

WELLS AND DALE

Once there were two villages, the village of Wells and the village of Dale. They stood side by side in the forest, but the people were always quarrelling. They would accuse each other of stealing and cheating and causing trouble, and sometimes their quarrels would break into fights.

This went on for year after year until, one day, it got so bad that the people of Wells attacked the Dale folk and drove them out. They set light to their houses and trampled their gardens and pulled up their crops. Some Dale folk were killed, and the rest ran away into the forest.

'Drive them out!' shouted the Wells folk. 'We're better without them. Send them away!' And they drove great stakes into the soil all around Dale to close it off.

Only afterwards, as Dale lay in ruins, did they discover that something terrible had happened. A group of Wells children had been playing in Dale, and had been caught up in the fighting and killed.

The people of Wells were devastated. They could not speak of what had happened, and they tried to hide their faces from each other. Instead of rejoicing that their enemies had gone, they were heavy-hearted and ashamed.

Dale village lay empty and desolate for years. It was a place of shadows and cold mists. No birds sang in the trees. No plants grew. The rain refused to fall on the soil, and the sun refused to shine.

One day, an old Wells woman left her village and climbed in through the fence, and looked about her. She was the mother of one of the children who had been killed.

She walked about and gazed at the dead ground and the broken houses. She sat in the village centre and remembered what it had been like when it was full of people, living and working and trading and raising their children, just like in her own village. And she thought of the loss to both villages.

In her mind she imagined the sound of children playing—and then the sound grew louder, and she realized it was real. Two boys and a girl were running and playing among the sticks and rubble. A young man appeared and called their names. He saw the old woman and came towards her. She stood up, ready to run if need be.

'You used to live here, didn't you?' she said boldly. 'This is your village.'

'No,' he replied. 'I used to play here. I and my friends. I lived in the next village.'

She stared at his face, and a sudden thought gripped her heart. 'What happened?' she whispered.

'There was a terrible battle. My friends were killed. The Dale folk took me with them, and we fled into the forest.'

The woman lifted her hands towards him. 'My son!' she cried.

Her tears fell on to the earth and blessed it. As mother and son held each other, the children drew closer. 'These are your grandchildren,' he told her.

Over the next few weeks, the people of Wells helped the young man to pull out all the stakes around the village. He and his family moved in and began to repair the houses.

The Dale folk started to return, and the people of Wells lent them tools and gave them seeds to grow crops, and promised to help with the harvest.

'One of our sons has come back from the dead,' the Wells folk told them. 'And now he has become your son as well. From now on, our lives are bound together.'

And from all the surrounding trees, the song of the birds rose into the open sky.

> **Peace will last for ever.** ISAIAH 9:7

BIBLE REFERENCES

Isaiah 9:2–7; Luke 9:51–56; Colossians 1:19–23; James 4:1–6

SERMON POINTERS

★ **Isaiah 9:2–7:** What is the context for peace in this prophecy? What expectations do we have for world peace?

★ **Luke 9:51–56:** What would the correction they received have taught James and John about their attitude to the Samaritans? What would it have taught them about the work of Jesus?

★ **Colossians 1:19–23:** What do we learn about the peace process that God has implemented? How can we remain firm in our faith?

★ **James 4:1–6:** What is the tension that James is exploring here? How can we live at peace with each other? What does it mean to be a friend of the world?

QUESTIONS FOR YOUNGER LISTENERS

★ What caused the two villages to fight each other?

★ What did the old woman think about as she looked at the empty village?

★ In what sense did her son belong to both villages?

★ How does Jesus bring peace into the world?

★ How can we live at peace with each other?

VISUAL AIDS AND ACTIONS

★ Paper chains

Give each child a piece of paper chain to write their name on. Write 'Jesus' on one as well. Then ask the children to add their piece to the chain, and close the circle with the name of Jesus.

THE MONSTER

Once there was a monster who lived in a deep cave under a hill. The people who lived in the nearby village were frightened of him and hated him. The shepherds were sure he stole their newborn lambs. Sometimes they would find only hooves or a strip of fleece where the lamb had been.

The monster didn't know that the villagers hated him. In fact, he didn't know he was a monster until, one day, he saw some children playing up on the hillside. The monster was very shy so he didn't go too close. He would never have hurt them. He wasn't that kind of monster. But directly they saw him, the children shrieked and ran away and told their father. That night, a group of men came tramping over the ground towards the cave. They were carrying bracken and twigs and branches, anything that would burn, and they piled it high on the earth outside the entrance and set light to it.

The monster coughed in a puzzled way, and hid further in the cave. 'Burn, monster, burn!' shouted the villagers. The monster sat quietly till they had gone, and then stomped out the burning ashes with his big feet.

Now the children's father was a shepherd. One night, he was out looking for a sheep that had strayed away from the flock. He thought perhaps the monster had taken her, or perhaps she had fallen into a gully and hurt herself. The shepherd listened for the sound of her bleating, but heard nothing.

Then, in the dark, his foot slipped, and he found himself tumbling down and down the hillside and landing by a great rock. He could tell his leg was broken, and his back ached. He lay there, cold and in pain, for some hours. Then he heard a snuffling sound. He thought it might be the missing sheep, but it wasn't. It was the monster. Far above him, two moonlit eyes peered down and a great mouth fell open.

The shepherd was terrified, but he was also filled with hatred for the monster. 'Get on with it,' he cried. 'Eat me if you're going to.'

The monster knelt down, sniffed the shepherd, stretched out two huge arms and lifted him up. The shepherd fainted with pain and fear. When he came round, he was lying warm and snug among the sheep in his own sheep-pen, which is where his family found him the next morning.

The shepherd never told anyone how he'd got down the mountainside with a broken leg. The lost sheep was never found, but when his children said, 'I bet the monster ate her,' he would say, 'Probably a wolf, or an eagle. Those monster stories, you don't want to believe everything people say.' Whenever the villagers wanted to hunt the monster down, the shepherd would persuade them it was a waste of time, and they'd far better get back to their work or their families.

So the monster went on living in his cave, and sharing his shelter was the missing sheep, who trotted in and out and nibbled the green grass that grew so freshly out of the scorched soil.

> **'Now I am certain that God treats all people alike.'**
> ACTS 10:34

BIBLE REFERENCES

Isaiah 56:1–8; Luke 10:25–37; Acts 10:27–36; Romans 15:7–13

SERMON POINTERS

* **Isaiah 56:1–8:** What vision does Isaiah give us of salvation? Who is it for?
* **Luke 10:25–37:** Does the story instruct us to love those in need, or the Samaritans? Who are the 'Samaritans' in our lives and culture?

* **Acts 10:27–36**: Are we ever surprised at the people whom God asks to be his followers? Do we present the gospel as only for the kind of people we are?
* **Romans 15:7–13**: Do we have an equivalent divide to the one between Jews and Gentiles? How can we apply this teaching in our lives?

QUESTIONS FOR YOUNGER LISTENERS

* Why did the villagers hate the monster?
* Did the monster deserve to be hated?
* Why did Jesus tell us to love our enemies?
* How did the monster show love to his enemies?

VISUAL AIDS AND ACTIONS

* Paper

Crumple some paper for sound effect as you cry, 'Burn, monster, burn!' The children might do this with you.

MORGAN THE PUPPETEER

There was one thing that Morgan's father said to her nearly every day: 'Puppets aren't real, you know.'

Morgan spent so much time working with her puppets that he worried about her.

'What about your school work?' he said. 'Are you doing your homework? Puppets aren't real, you know.'

'I know,' she said.

Morgan had six puppets. They were very old, and were dressed in medieval costume. There was a gipsy girl and a gipsy boy, a richly dressed man with a purse of gold, and an old woman twining wool for weaving. Morgan's favourites were a young girl in peacock blue and crimson, and a young man playing a flute. Each of them had a set of coloured strings, so that she could move their arms and legs, turn their heads and make them dance.

'Puppets aren't people, you know,' said her father. 'Why don't you find yourself some real friends?'

But Morgan wasn't good at making friends. She never knew what to say. She did have one friend—an old lady, Miss Gable, who lived across the road in a house as ancient as herself. The garden was overgrown and full of weeds, and birds would gather in the trees from dawn till dusk. Her father didn't like her visiting the old lady, but he knew she was harmless.

Miss Gable had a secret that only Morgan knew. When she had been very young, she had been on the stage, and she told Morgan many wonderful stories of the life she had led.

'I'd like to put on a play,' said Morgan. 'A puppet play.'

'Then you must do it,' replied Miss Gable. 'You can invite your friends, and I shall invite some of mine. We'll have it in the garden.'

'I haven't got any friends,' Morgan told her. 'Only you.'

'Then this is the way to make them,' said Miss Gable. 'Plays draw people together.'

She told Morgan the plot of a play she had been in as a young girl, and Morgan wanted to use it. At first, Morgan's father wasn't keen.

'I keep telling her,' he said to Miss Gable. 'Puppets aren't real.'

'No,' said Miss Gable. 'But they show us what *we* are like, and that makes *us* more real.'

So, one Saturday night, Morgan put on her play. She'd asked some children from school to make the scenery and sell tickets, and her father had cut the grass. One boy had even offered to help her work the puppets. In the end, there were several children in the audience, two or three neighbours, some very strange friends of Miss Gable, and Morgan's father.

Morgan was so nervous that she tangled up the strings on the two gipsies as they came on stage. Someone coughed, and someone else laughed.

'This is a tale,' she began, 'of the Black Death, and how the plague was carried from village to village by those trying to escape it—until a group of people chose to sacrifice their lives so that the disease would travel no further.'

As the play unfolded, something happened to Morgan. She felt braver and braver—not only about the play, but about everything. She thought of all the children who'd helped put on the play. Miss Gable was right, the puppets did make everyone more real, and for the first time she felt she belonged.

You find families for those who are lonely. PSALM 68:6

BIBLE REFERENCES

Ezra 1:1–6; Psalm 68:5–6; John 17:20–23; 1 Corinthians 12:4–13

SERMON POINTERS

★ **Ezra 1:1–6:** In what ways did people contribute to the project? What projects bring people together in your church? What are the different skills and gifts they employ?

★ **Psalm 68:5–6:** How do these verses endorse the value of friendship and community? What does the opposite image imply?

★ **John 17:20–23:** Why does Jesus pray this for his followers? How can we become the united community that God intends?

★ **1 Corinthians 12:4–13:** How can we help each other discover the special gifts God has given us? Do we value some gifts above others? Is this consistent with being a united body?

QUESTIONS FOR YOUNGER LISTENERS

★ Why did Morgan find it hard to make friends?
★ How did Miss Gable show friendship to Morgan?
★ How did Morgan's play bring people together?
★ How does Christianity bring people together today?

VISUAL AIDS AND ACTIONS

★ A selection of puppets

Introduce the puppets to the children and have them ask each other questions.

‡

THE ALIEN AND THE RUGBY BALL

Martin was kicking a rugby ball over the bar in the park when he saw an alien spaceship land in the duck pond. The spaceship disappeared under water. Martin went over to have a look. The spaceship came back to the surface, and bobbed about gently. A hatch opened and out crawled a small alien. It was talking into a handset.

'Report update… Surface of planet very soft. Will not sustain walking.'

'You're in the pond!' called Martin.

'Report update… Have landed on planet called Pond.'

A duck swam up to the alien spacecraft and started eating some of the weeds that had been dragged up from the bottom.

Martin pointed to the pathway. 'Step out here—it's quite firm.'

The alien looked at him for a moment and then sprang on to the earth. 'Aaah. Report update…'

'Never mind that,' said Martin. 'What are you doing here?'

'Research.' The alien turned round and started talking to the duck. They seemed to get on quite well, so Martin went back to kicking the rugby ball.

After a while he heard a voice behind him. 'Report update… Planet creature trying to break open large egg with foot.'

Martin laughed. 'It's a rugby ball,' he said. 'It's a game. I'm just practising.'

'Question. Why not reverse gravity to allow ball to fly?'

'Reverse it?' said Martin. 'What are you talking about? Gravity doesn't reverse.'

The alien was very alarmed and began clicking his handset. 'Report update… Have just learnt… gravity on planet earth cannot be reversed. Question. How am I going to get back into space?'

'You'll have to stay here.' Martin turned round and kicked the ball again. It sailed up, bounced off the crossbar and went the wrong side of the post.

'This planet is no good for our people,' said the alien mournfully. 'And now I can never leave it. Goodbye, friends.' He switched off the handset and went and sat dejectedly on the grass.

Martin began to feel sorry for him. 'Here, have a sandwich,' he said, opening his packed lunch. 'You can live with us, if you like. My brother's leaving home soon. You can have his room.'

The alien tried to smile. 'You are so kind. But I have a home, and I will miss it. Is there no way you can reverse gravity here?'

'Let's take a look at this spacecraft of yours.' They wandered back to the duck pond and found a dragonfly perched on the hatch cover. Martin leaned over and picked the spacecraft out of the water. 'It's very light,' he said, turning it over. 'Don't you have rockets? To launch yourself into space?'

'No,' said the alien. 'We don't need rockets, we just reverse a bit of gravity. The engine does the rest.'

Martin bounced the spaceship up in the air and caught it a couple of times. 'How fast would it have to go before the engines took over?'

The alien did some calculations on his handset.

'Let me see... travelling at XY speed, times ten, for two seconds, plus samples of duckweed and earth soil... Um, about the same speed as your egg.'

'Egg? The rugby ball?' Martin smiled. 'Come on, then, let's see if it works.'

On the edge of the pitch, the alien climbed into the spacecraft, and Martin carefully placed it on the ground in front of the posts.

'Goodbye,' said the alien. 'You have been a good friend. If you ever come to my planet, you will be welcome.'

Martin concentrated, then swung his leg and kicked the spacecraft as hard as he could. It sailed up into the air, straight over the bar, then shot upwards so rapidly that Martin blinked and it had gone. He heard the crowd go wild, but it may just have been the ducks on the pond, quacking.

> 'When I was a stranger you welcomed me.' MATTHEW 25:35

BIBLE REFERENCES

Genesis 18:1–8; Matthew 25:31–36; Hebrews 13:1–3; 3 John 5–8

SERMON POINTERS

* **Genesis 18:1–8**: Why was Abraham so welcoming? Do we serve our guests with such honour?
* **Matthew 25:31–36**: Who are the 'strangers' today? Do we welcome people as we would Christ? What prevents us?
* **Hebrews 13:1–3**: Are these strangers fellow believers? Why is hospitality given such importance? What part does it have in the gospel?
* **3 John 5–8**: There are strangers today travelling in the Lord's service. Are we willing to help them in their work? How can we tell whom to trust?

QUESTIONS FOR YOUNGER LISTENERS

* How did Martin offer help to the alien?
* What help did the alien need?
* What promise did the alien make to Martin?
* What does Jesus say about showing friendship to those in need?
* How can we show friendship to others?

VISUAL AIDS AND ACTIONS

✱ A rugby ball

Ask if anyone plays rugby, and if they know how rugby started. (Supposedly, William Webb Ellis, playing football at Rugby School in 1823, picked up the ball and ran with it.)

THE BLACK STONE

Hundreds of years ago, a boy called Luke lived in a village in Gloucestershire. His older brother, Adam, was an explorer, and had crossed the seas many times and visited many countries. Once he had travelled as far as China, and had been away for nearly five years. He always brought back exciting and colourful objects from his travels, and had many tales to tell.

'Next time I come back,' he told Luke, 'I'll bring you a special present. You'll be twelve soon, and no longer a child.'

Luke waited every day for his brother to return. He tried to imagine what the gift might be. Perhaps a silver dagger with a carved ivory sheath; perhaps a many-coloured bird that he could teach to speak—or something even better.

One day, a stranger came to the house and asked for Master Luke. 'From your brother Adam,' the man told him, handing him a package. 'He is delayed in travelling, but he sends you this present.'

The man went indoors to speak to Luke's parents, and Luke carried the bundle away from the house. He could hardly wait to open it. It was quite heavy, but had no particular shape. Swiftly he untied the piece of leather cloth, opened it out, and there in his hand lay a rough black stone.

Luke stared in dismay. Was that it? A stone? An ugly old stone? He felt like flinging it down the well, or away from him into the long grass. He was angry but he was also puzzled. Surely his brother wasn't playing a trick on him? He began to think that there might be a jewel inside, or even gold. Or perhaps the stone was magic. Luke wrapped it up again in the leather cloth and hid it under his bedclothes.

It was three weeks before Adam returned. He looked older and his skin was toughened by the sea and the sun. Luke was overjoyed to see him, and forgot the strange present, wanting to hear all his brother's adventures. Adam talked late into the night, until Luke's eyelids fell shut and his mother sent him to bed.

Early next morning, Luke woke to see his brother smiling down at him.

'Did you like my present?' he asked.

'The stone? It was... yes, thank you.'

Adam laughed. 'You don't know what it is, do you?' he said.

'Is it gold?' asked Luke.

'It's a lodestone. Don't you remember? I told you that sailors use them for finding their way across the seas. Fetch me the stone.' Luke reached under the bedding and gave it to his brother.

Adam took a long needle from his purse. To Luke's amazement, the needle sprang from his brother's fingers and fastened itself to the rock. Adam stroked the needle several times against the stone, and handed it to Luke. 'There. Now float the needle on a piece of cork and it will point to the north. Wherever you are, wherever you go, for the rest of your life, this stone will help to guide you.'

Adam held the stone, his eyes bright. He felt as if a whole world of adventure and discovery had opened up to him. 'It *is* magic,' he breathed. 'I nearly threw it away. And it's the best present I've ever had.'

> 'The Spirit shows what is true and will come and guide you into the full truth.' JOHN 16:13

BIBLE REFERENCES

Exodus 13:20–22; John 16:12–15; Acts 8:26–39; Romans 8:26–27

SERMON POINTERS

✱ **Exodus 13:20–22:** What do we understand by the cloud and the fire? Why are we told that God was 'in' them?

* **John 16:12–15:** How is the promised gift of the Holy Spirit to guide the disciples? What is the role of the Holy Spirit in relation to Jesus?
* **Acts 8:26–39:** In what ways did the Holy Spirit guide Philip in these verses? Do we experience the Holy Spirit leading us to work for God's purposes?
* **Romans 8:26–27:** How does the Holy Spirit help us to communicate with God? What do we learn about the role and nature of the Holy Spirit in these verses?

QUESTIONS FOR YOUNGER LISTENERS

* What is lodestone? *(Its other name is magnetite)*
* Why did Luke nearly throw it away?
* Why was he so excited when he found out what it could do?
* How does God's Holy Spirit guide us?
* How does God's Holy Spirit help us to pray?

VISUAL AIDS AND ACTIONS

* A compass
* A magnet and a needle

Ask the children to point to the north, south, east and west. Show them how the needle can be magnetized.

THE OLD DRAGON

Every morning at six o'clock, *The Old Dragon* would be filled up with coal and water, and then shunted out to wait alongside the platform for the morning passengers. Sam Barr was the engine driver, and had been for thirty years. Twice a day he'd drive her up the mountain to the station and then down again after a two-hour break. There was only one coach, filled with walkers and climbers and sightseers and some workmen who were building a mountain station higher up.

Most days, Sam had a stoker with him who would heave coal into the fire and keep the steam pressure high. It was slow work going up the mountain, for *The Old Dragon* needed all her strength to push the coach up safely. Sam loved his job. He even loved caring for the engine, polishing the brass and oiling all the workings.

Not everyone understood, though. The mountain station had a helicopter landing site, so that important people could be whisked up there to see how the work was going. Joe was the helicopter pilot, and he never lost a chance to mock Sam for his love of engines.

'Running on tracks,' he'd say. 'That's dull. No fun in that. A helicopter's like a bird. I can go where I like.'

'You've got tracks,' said Sam. 'You just can't see them.'

Joe would laugh and offer to take Sam up in his helicopter to see how much fun it was.

But to Sam nothing could beat the feel of an engine gathering strength, or the smell of the hot oil and burning coal, or the sound of the pistons or the whistle as they came near the platform. And if the track were the same day after day, what did it matter?

He loved the changing mountainside—white in winter, fresh green as the spring came, and blazing with colour in the summer and autumn. Every day was new to him, and it was never dull.

One morning Sam woke early, around four o'clock. He could hear voices outside. He pulled on a coat and went to the door. The air was thick with fog and he could just make out four men. He recognized them as workmen from the mountain station.

'Who's there?' he called. 'What's up?'

'The helicopter's missing,' said one. 'It set off from the station last night but never got back. Trouble is, with this fog, we can't send anyone up to look for it.'

'*The Old Dragon* can go,' said Sam. 'Fog never bothered her.'

The men climbed on board, and took turns as stoker. Without her coach, *The Old Dragon* travelled faster. The men kept a lookout for signs of the helicopter. As they turned a bend where the mountain path narrowed, one of them shouted, 'There!'

Sam threw the brake and the old engine wheezed and squealed to a halt. They found Joe near the wreckage of his helicopter. He had a cut on his forehead and one arm was at a bad angle. They guessed he had climbed out after the crash, and then fainted.

A few days later, Sam visited him in hospital. Joe was sitting up, his head bandaged and his arm in plaster.

'Came off the rails, I see,' said Sam.

'You're right,' said Joe. 'I hit a tree in the fog.'

'Lucky you were near the track, or we'd never have found you.'

'That wasn't luck,' said Joe. 'I was following it down. It was the only way I could tell where I was.'

'Oh,' Sam smiled. 'Maybe there's use in those old rails after all.'

'Maybe,' said Joe.

> **You must never stop looking at the perfect law that sets you free.** JAMES 1:25

BIBLE REFERENCES

Micah 4:1–4; Matthew 22:34–40; 2 Timothy 3:14–17; James 1:22–25

SERMON POINTERS

* **Micah 4:1–4:** Micah's prophecy shows how the law has a place in God's future kingdom. What is its place?
* **Matthew 22:34–40:** Was Jesus giving a new teaching? Or was he radically transforming the teaching they already held?
* **2 Timothy 3:14–17:** What are the purposes of scripture as seen in these verses? How can we better ensure its place in our lives?
* **James 1:22–25:** What is the law that gives freedom? How can freedom and law go together? How obedient are we to God's message?

QUESTIONS FOR YOUNGER LISTENERS

* What did Sam and Joe each feel about the railway?
* How did the tracks help Joe in the fog?
* What other kinds of tracks might people need in their lives—visible or invisible?
* What kind of tracks has God given us?
* What happens if we use them, or don't use them?

VISUAL AIDS AND ACTIONS

* Four empty bottles

Blow across the top of a bottle to produce a steady note. Better still, use four different bottles simultaneously and get the children to produce the effect of a steam whistle.

HARBOUR LIGHTS

Long ago, before ships had radar or sonar to guide them into safe waters, sailors used to rely on landmarks during the day and special lights at night. This is the story of a small merchant ship finding its way into a strange harbour after weeks at sea. The master of the ship was called Walter Bates, and his uncle owned the shipping line. Some people said that the only reason Walter had been made master was because of his uncle.

⁘

The ship had been forced off course by bad weather, and was sailing towards a harbour sheltered from the wind. Night was falling. The navigator with his charts warned them that there were many rocks, and they needed to find the entrance to the channel which would lead them into harbour. Either side of the channel, there would be a light, a beacon, kept burning every night to guide them through.

Walter stood on the deck, feeling the force of the wind and rain, his eyes straining for the two lights. Suddenly the wind gathered strength, and the mate, Barnabas Nye, shouted to the men to haul tighter on the ropes to keep the ship on course.

'Channel ahead,' called the lookout. Walter peered through the rain and saw two lights glimmering in the distance. He realized with a shock that the ship had veered off course, and he shouted the order to go ten degrees to port. He sensed the sailors muttering around him that he was too new to the job.

'Sir, beggin' your pardon, sir,' said the voice of an old seaman.

'Yes, what is it?' he answered.

'Something's wrong, sir.'

Walter wondered if the man was insulting him. 'There's nothing wrong, sailor. The channel lights are ahead of us.'

'Sir,' the old man insisted. 'I know these waters. I was raised here. The lights are wrong. The channel's to starboard. I know it.'

Walter felt alarmed. If the sailor was right, the ship was heading straight for the rocks. On such a wild night, they would all be lost. He turned to Barnabas. 'What do you make of it?'

'Get back to work, Lucas, you've gone feeble,' snapped the mate.

The old man turned away. Walter watched him, and then called out, 'Why? Why would the lights be wrong? Who would change them?'

The word came back to him in the darkness. 'Wreckers.'

Walter felt a grip of fear. Wreckers—people who deliberately made a ship hit the rocks so that they could plunder its goods and kill the crew.

So who was he to trust? An old sailor who knew the sea, or the two guiding lights he could see ahead of him? He reached a decision and gave his instructions.

The ship changed course again, sailing for the far side of one of the lights. The sailors were uneasy and mistrustful. With beating hearts they neared the light and sailed past it, leaving it to port. And as they did so, suddenly there was a flicker and a splutter and a light blazed on their starboard side. The figure of the coastguard could be seen with two other men, relighting the beacon that the wreckers had put out.

Walter felt a great wave of relief and thanks. The old sailor had been right, and he'd been right to trust him.

The ship sailed up the channel into harbour, and the old sailor, Lucas, went ashore with special leave to visit his family. There was not a man aboard who did not think he deserved it.

> **'Many false prophets will come and fool a lot of people.'**
> MATTHEW 24:11

BIBLE REFERENCES

1 Kings 22:10–18; Matthew 24:1–14; 2 Peter 2:1–3; 2 John 7–11

SERMON POINTERS

✱ **1 Kings 22:10–18**: What pressure was Micaiah under to say what Ahab wanted to hear? In what ways do we give in to similar pressure?

✱ **Matthew 24:1–14**: Is Jesus trying to distress his disciples, or to protect them? How can we help each other to be faithful to the end?

✱ **2 Peter 2:1–3**: How might we be cheated by false teaching? How can we test whether someone's message is false?

✱ **2 John 7–11**: Why does John speak so harshly about those with different theological beliefs? What is he warning his readers?

QUESTIONS FOR YOUNGER LISTENERS

✱ What choice did Walter have to make?
✱ Why was Lucas so worried?
✱ What would have happened if Walter had ignored him?
✱ When did he know he'd made the right choice?
✱ How can we tell if someone is teaching untrue things about God?

VISUAL AIDS AND ACTIONS

✱ The words 'port' and 'starboard' written out on separate pieces of card

Teach the children that port is left and starboard is right. Call out 'port' and 'starboard' and get them to point, till they get it right.

THE ROBIN IN THE GREENHOUSE

One day, Bertie the robin flew through the open doorway of a greenhouse. He didn't know he was in a greenhouse because he didn't understand about glass. He just kept flying until 'bump', some invisible wall seemed to be there in front of him.

Bertie felt a bit dazed but darted to one side and tried again. Bump. He tried flying higher and hit himself against the roof. Bump.

In a panic, Bertie fluttered about and perched on one of the window frames, then hovered in front of the glass trying to push his way through. 'Something's wrong with the air,' he thought. 'It's gone solid.'

Bertie began to feel weak and faint. He tried flying as fast as he could, but only battered himself till he was even more giddy.

A voice called out, 'Polly! Polly, come quickly!' The voice belonged to an old lady called Dorothy. Dorothy had been gardening and was putting her flowerpots back in the greenhouse when she saw the little bird. He was crouched, all ruffled and frightened, in one corner of a window pane. 'Look, we must rescue it, poor thing.'

'Oh dear, yes,' said her sister. 'Try waving a newspaper.'

They tried everything—catching him in a flowerpot, waving him towards the door, putting bread out on the pathway—but nothing worked.

'He still thinks he can get through the glass,' said Polly. 'We don't want to frighten him any more or he'll die of shock.'

Then Dorothy had an idea. They both went outside. Polly stood one side of the greenhouse, while Dorothy stood the other. Then Dorothy reached out her hand towards the little robin, and he shifted away from her. Again she moved her hand, pressed flat against the pane, and Bertie moved as well, trying to get round her.

'It's working!' called Polly. Carefully, Dorothy guided him along the side of the greenhouse. Every time he tried to fly past her hand, she moved it over, edging him closer and closer to the door.

'I wish she'd get out of the way,' grumbled Bertie to himself. 'She keeps stopping me. I suppose she wants to keep me here and eat me.' He came to the corner of the greenhouse, and Dorothy followed him, her hand still flat against the glass.

'She's very slow,' he thought. 'It must be because she's so old.' He made one last effort to get round her, and this time she didn't move.

'Done it!' he sang, and flew through the doorway, up into the air and on to the fence.

'He's free!' cried Polly. 'Well done, Dorothy!'

'Silly thing!' said her sister. 'I hope he has more sense next time.' And she went back into the greenhouse to collect her spade and fork.

Bertie watched her digging, his head on one side. He still wasn't quite sure whether she could be trusted, but he was sure that some of the worms she was digging up looked very tasty indeed.

> **The Holy Spirit would not let them preach in Asia.** ACTS 16:6

BIBLE REFERENCES

Numbers 22:22–35; Jonah 4:1–11; Matthew 16:21–26; Acts 16:6–15

SERMON POINTERS

✷ **Numbers 22:22–35:** Are we angry when our plans are thwarted? Do we recognize when God is saying 'no'? What mercy did God show in this story?

✳ **Jonah 4:1–11:** Why was Jonah so angry? Was God teasing and tormenting him, or teaching him? How do we respond to irritation?

✳ **Matthew 16:21–26:** Was Peter acting in good faith? Why did Jesus react so strongly? What assumptions do we make that might hinder God's purposes?

✳ **Acts 16:6–15:** Paul was prevented from going to Asia. Would we have been quicker to see this as the work of the enemy rather than the Holy Spirit? What new way opened up for Paul's team and what were the consequences?

QUESTIONS FOR YOUNGER LISTENERS

✳ How do you think Bertie felt about the glass?

✳ Do you think he needed help to get free?

✳ Did he recognize help when it came? What did he think Dorothy was doing?

✳ Does God stop us or say 'no' to us sometimes?

✳ Why does he?

VISUAL AIDS AND ACTIONS

✳ A 'No entry' sign

Ask the children what the 'No entry' sign means and why it is used. Or, if you know a mime artist, ask them to demonstrate trying to get out of a glass house.

THE ISLAND

Greg looked at his uncle's map. 'That's odd,' he said. 'The path just stops.'

Paula took the map. 'It led us down to the beach,' she said. 'We can't have gone wrong.'

'It's an old map.' Greg shifted the straps on his rucksack. 'Come on, we'll have to find our own way.'

Paula sighed. Going on holiday to an island sounded fun, but it was beginning to be a trial. Their uncle was an artist and he'd hired a house so that he could paint. But the house was on the far side of the island and there were no roads. All they had was the map that he'd sent them, and it did look very old.

'Hey, look, someone's fishing.' Paula pointed to a boy standing on the rocks with a fishing rod, and a satchel on his back.

'Can you tell us the way off the beach?' called Greg. 'We need to cross the island.'

'Sure.' The boy reeled in his line and dismantled the rod. 'Follow me.'

He led them to the mouth of a cave, and they followed him inside. It grew darker and there was a smell of damp and seaweed. Paula hoped the boy knew what he was doing. The tide was beginning to turn, and would soon fill the cave. But then she felt a slight breeze touch her face, and a glow of light shone ahead. There was a gap in the rocks at the back of the cave, leading up to a pathway. They climbed out on to the cliff top.

'Thanks,' Greg said to the boy. 'We'd never have found it. It's not on the map.'

'The map's fine,' replied the boy.

Greg and Paula looked again, and saw that he was right. A faint line led into the cave and out beyond it.

'It's easy to miss,' said the boy, and then he added, 'You're limping.'

'Yes, I twisted my ankle getting off the boat.' Greg didn't want to admit that it was beginning to hurt a lot.

'I didn't know,' Paula frowned. 'Do you need a stick or something?'

'No, I'm OK, come on.'

They walked along the coastal path leading around the cliff face. Paula looked back.

'The boy's standing by that path up to the woods,' she said. 'Should we follow him? He seems to know the island.'

'No,' said Greg. 'This way's fine. We've got the map. We don't need him.'

They turned the corner and stopped. The path before them had disappeared. Great chunks of cliff face had broken off and fallen into the sea, eroded by the wind and waves.

'Ah,' said Greg. 'We'll go the other way.'

The boy was waiting for them by the path to the woods. As they walked uphill, Paula noticed that the boy was carrying Greg's rucksack, and that Greg was looking pale. 'Is it much farther?' she asked.

'A bit,' said the boy. 'We can rest here for a minute.'

As they rested, the boy bound up Greg's ankle with the strap from his satchel. 'That feels better,' said Greg. 'Thanks.'

From there they soon reached the ridge. The house stood in a hollow on the hillside some way below them.

'We made it!' cried Paula, starting downhill.

Greg turned to the boy. 'You've been a great help,' he said.

As the boy walked away, Paula called after him. 'Where are you going?'

The boy smiled. 'Fishing, of course,' he called back. 'I'm going fishing.'

'I will be with you always, even until the end of the world.'
MATTHEW 28:20

BIBLE REFERENCES

Exodus 33:1–23; Matthew 28:16–20; Mark 1:14–20; John 14:15–21

SERMON POINTERS

* **Exodus 33:1–23**: Why was it so important to Moses that God should not leave them? Would the promised land still have been theirs? Do we focus on God's gifts, and forget him?
* **Matthew 28:16–20**: How do the promise and the instruction link together? Are we inclined to dwell on one rather than the other?
* **Mark 1:14–20**: What was Jesus asking the fishermen to do? What did he promise them? Why was it important that they went with him?
* **John 14:15–21**: What comfort is Jesus offering his disciples? What is he asking them to do? In what way is God present with us?

QUESTIONS FOR YOUNGER LISTENERS

* Where were Greg and Paula going?
* Why did they need the map?
* Why was the boy more help than a map?
* What does Jesus promise his disciples?
* How does Jesus help us day by day?

VISUAL AIDS AND ACTIONS

* Map
* Strong boots
* Stick
* Water bottle

Ask what else you might need on a long walk.

THE HOT AIR BALLOON

The animals in the fields looked up as a huge hot air balloon passed over their heads. There were three children and a man in the basket hanging under the balloon. The man was half-lying, half-sitting, his face very pale, nursing one of his arms. The oldest girl was called Emily, and it had been her idea to travel by balloon.

'It's the best way to get home, Dad,' said Emily. 'We can fly the balloon. You've often shown us how it works. And the wind's in the right direction.'

They'd been travelling in their father's truck with the balloon in its special trailer, on their way to a showground where their father gave rides to people for money. But then it had all gone wrong. Somewhere along the mountain road, the truck had swerved to miss a pothole and crashed into the mountain wall. The children were unharmed but their father had broken his shoulder.

'You must do everything I say,' said their father. 'Otherwise it's too dangerous. Do you promise?' They all nodded. 'All right, then. Let's make a start.'

They laid out the balloon on the ground and attached it to the basket. A powerful fan began to inflate the balloon. Then they climbed into the basket and Emily fired up the burner. There was a loud whooshing noise as the balloon filled with warm air. 'Hang on tight,' she warned, and unfastened the ropes mooring them to the ground.

Slowly, the basket began lifting up into the sky. 'We're flying!' cried Jim. He looked at his father, who had slumped to the floor and was wincing with pain. Jim pulled a blanket out from a rucksack and spread it over him. The balloon bounced and shuddered as they moved away from the mountain air.

'Do you think we can fly all the way home?' asked Jim.

'I'm sure we can,' said Emily, trying to sound calm.

'I'm hungry,' grumbled Harriet, the youngest.

'We've got some biscuits.' Emily opened the tin and counted rapidly. 'There's two each. You can have one now and one later.'

'You sound like Mum,' said Jim.

Emily wished her mother was there with them. She tucked the blanket more firmly round her father. He stirred and opened his eyes.

Jim watched the clouds passing above their heads. 'You should always check the fuel and the weather before you set out. Isn't that right, Dad?'

His father smiled. 'That's right, son.'

They ate the biscuits. Their father gave one of his to Harriet, and Emily gave one of hers to Jim. 'Look!' cried Jim, suddenly. 'I can see the river.'

'Nearly home.' Their father struggled to his feet. 'Any power lines? No, that's OK.

You must always look out for power lines. Take her down, Em.'

Emily turned down the burner and the air in the balloon began to cool. As it did so, they started to come down.

The sun was setting as they sailed over their house and sank down into a field, dragging the basket over the soft earth. Seconds later, a farm truck came across the field towards them.

'Mrs Blake's children!' said the farmer in surprise. 'And Mr Blake! Why, you need to get to hospital.' He radioed his wife to arrange for an ambulance. 'What about the rest of you? Are you all right?'

'We had a good flight,' said Emily, helping Harriet out of the basket.

'You're just like your mother,' said the farmer. 'So sensible.'

Emily walked towards the truck, holding Harriet by the hand. Nobody noticed that her legs were wobbling like jelly.

Do as God does. EPHESIANS 5:1

BIBLE REFERENCES

Genesis 1:26–31; John 5:19–21; Ephesians 5:1–2;
1 Thessalonians 1:4–10

SERMON POINTERS

* **Genesis 1:26–31**: Why did God make us like himself? What does that mean for us today?
* **John 5:19–21**: Why is it significant that Jesus copied his father in everything? What does this tell us about our relationship with God?
* **Ephesians 5:1–2**: What is to guide our actions? How are we to discern what God would do?
* **1 Thessalonians 1:4–10**: How did the Thessalonians set a good example? How had they been set a good example? Is this how your church teaches?

QUESTIONS FOR YOUNGER LISTENERS

* Why did the children fly in the balloon?
* What did their father make them promise?
* Can you remember anything their father taught them?
* Why should we try to behave like Jesus?

VISUAL AIDS AND ACTIONS

Play 'Simon says'. The children copy a leader who begins each action by saying, 'Simon says do this'. If the leader only says, 'Do this' the children should do nothing.

❖

PODDLE THE WILDEBEEST

'That's right, Poddle, keep up!' said his mother.

'Where are we going?' wailed Poddle. But his mother ignored him. 'Where are we going?' he asked his cousins.

'Keep going, Poddle,' they replied.

'Where?' he repeated. But they ignored him.

'Straight on,' said his father. 'Good boy.'

'Dad,' he asked, 'where are we going?'

'Don't worry, we'll be there soon.'

'WHERE ARE WE GOING?!' he shouted at the top of his voice.

'Dear me, what a noise,' said his mother. 'Keep your voice down, do.'

'This is the right way,' said his father. 'There's no need to make a fuss.'

Poddle got slower and slower. He felt tired and cross. He tried to keep up, but soon his family were a long way ahead of him. The other wildebeest around him kept pushing him forward, and he kept dropping back.

'I don't think I can go any further,' he told the last group. 'I think I'll stay here.'

'You can't do that,' they said in horror. 'You mustn't be left behind.'

An elderly wildebeest moved over to him. 'Don't worry,' he said. 'He can keep me company. I'm not as fast as I used to be. We'll travel together.'

'I'm not going,' said Poddle, and stopped.

'Why not?' asked the elderly wildebeest.

'I don't see the point.'

'Really? Is it not clear to you?'

'No.'

The animal looked puzzled. 'You do *know* where we're going, don't you?'

'No!' said Poddle firmly. 'I don't know where we're going, and I don't know why we're going. No one will tell me.'

'Oh!' said the elderly wildebeest. 'That's the trouble. No one has bothered to explain. Well, we've plenty of time, so as we move along we'll talk, and I'll tell you.'

As they walked side by side, he started to explain: 'We are going to the great river. After we cross the river we will be in a land of sweet, fresh grass, where there will be food enough for everyone. It will not be easy. The river is full of crocodiles. But the smell of the earth and fresh grass will keep us going.'

Poddle remembered how he'd stood among the great herd of wildebeest grazing on the land, and found it more and more difficult to find food. He remembered how hungry he'd felt at times, and how the herd had become restless and eager to move.

Now at last he understood. They were moving towards a world of fresh grass. A distant roll of thunder came to their ears, and the herd galloped powerfully forward.

'Come on,' Poddle urged the elderly wildebeest. 'Don't get left behind!' And he ran ahead to join his cousins, as they followed the wonderful smell of rain in the air.

We hope for something we have not yet seen. ROMANS 8:25

BIBLE REFERENCES

Deuteronomy 34:1–8; Luke 9:22–27; Romans 8:18–25; Hebrews 11:11–16

SERMON POINTERS

* **Deuteronomy 34:1–8:** How did God keep his word to Abraham, Isaac and Jacob? What did Moses see? What 'promised land' has God shown us?

* **Luke 9:22–27:** How does Jesus say we are to follow him? What is he anticipating for himself? What is the outcome for himself and those who follow him?
* **Romans 8:18–25:** In what way is creation to participate in God's plan for the future? What is the hope that saves us? Are we motivated by what awaits us?
* **Hebrews 11:11–16:** In what way did Abraham's descendants feel only strangers on earth? Where did they truly belong? What part did faith play?

QUESTIONS FOR YOUNGER LISTENERS

* What did Poddle want to know?
* What did he feel when no one told him?
* How did he feel when the elderly wildebeest did tell him?
* What has God promised us in the future?
* How do we know we will share in it?

VISUAL AIDS AND ACTIONS

* Coconut shells
* Blocks of wood
* A tray of gravel
* Tape recorder (optional)

Try to make the sound effects of stampeding wildebeest. If you have a tape recorder, record the results and play them while telling the story.

❖

CROSSING THE CAUSEWAY

Once there was a young girl called Fay, who lived on a small farm with her brothers and sisters. Every day she would milk the cow, collect the eggs, churn the butter, take her brothers and sisters to school and bake pies for their supper.

Some years before, a young man had passed through the village and stopped at the farm to buy some eggs. He had been on his way to the city, where he told her he had important work to do. They had talked together for a long time, and were so caught up in their conversation that she had forgotten to fetch him the eggs.

'Who are you?' she asked him as he turned to go.

'My name is Cullin,' he told her. 'I live in a castle far away where the day breaks and the shadows flee, and where my father is king. One day I will take you there, and we will be together for ever.'

The years passed by and Fay never forgot her friend, though she wondered if he had forgotten her. One day, to her joy, she received an invitation to a great feast at the prince's castle. She longed to see him again, so she set out towards the rising sun, where the day breaks and the shadows flee. She travelled for hours and days, for days and weeks, till she glimpsed ahead of her the golden turrets of a great castle.

Then, to her dismay, she saw that there was a wide stretch of sea dividing her from the island, and the waters before her feet looked dark and deep. 'How am I going to get across?' she wondered. There was no boat moored nearby, and no bridge. But a signpost, wedged deep into the sand, read, 'Causeway—cross here.'

For the first time she noticed a stone path, level with the water, stretching out across to the island. Cautiously she stepped on to the first stone, and the waves lapped against her ankles, startling her. Before long, a mist had blown in from the sea and covered the island, so she could no longer make out any sign of the castle.

Fay kept on walking, and the mist gathered around her till she could see neither in front of her nor behind. The roar of the waves grew in her ears and she began to feel giddy and cold. She was afraid of stepping off the causeway and falling into the water. 'If I fall, I'll be swept away and lost,' she thought.

Looking down, she could see strange shapes in the water, moving and gathering under the surface. She sensed that they were trying to draw her away with them. 'Come with us,' they seemed to say. 'It is peaceful here. You will float away and be part of the great sea for ever...'

For a moment Fay hesitated, and then she heard a voice calling her name through the mist. 'I'm here,' she cried. 'Where are you?'

A hand reached out and took her hand, and a voice close by said, 'Don't be afraid. Did you think I would let you make this crossing on your own?'

And there was her friend Cullin, his face kinder and more loving than she had ever remembered him. Together they walked side by side over the causeway until suddenly the mist cleared and there was the island, with the stone walls of the castle gleaming like gold in the sun. From within came the sounds of celebration, music and dancing and laughing voices.

'It is to welcome you,' he smiled as he led her in through the gates. 'And because this is our wedding day.'

> **I may walk through valleys as dark as death, but I won't be afraid.** PSALM 23:4

BIBLE REFERENCES

Psalm 23; John 14:1–3; Romans 8:35–39; Revelation 19:6–9

SERMON POINTERS

* **Psalm 23:** Why is this psalm often read at funerals? What comfort does it hold for those facing death?

* **John 14:1–3**: Why were the disciples worried? What did Jesus want them to understand about their future? What comfort do you find in his words?
* **Romans 8:35–39**: Again, what comfort do you find in these words? How does the love of Christ reach us, even in death? What is the victory we have won?
* **Revelation 19:6–9**: How do these images of marriage and celebration fit our understanding of life beyond death? Are they more physical, more relational, more exuberant than we sometimes imagine?

QUESTIONS FOR YOUNGER LISTENERS

* Why was Fay afraid of the sea around the island?
* When did she stop being afraid?
* Do we believe that Jesus is with us all the time, whatever we go through?
* What did Jesus tell his disciples would happen after they died?
* How do you think Fay felt about the welcome she received when she reached the castle?

VISUAL AIDS AND ACTIONS

* Half-filled bottles of water
* Squeaky plastic toys
* A tape recorder (optional)

Get the children to make sound effects of seagulls, the wind, waves on the shore and water splashing. If you have a tape recorder, record the sounds and play the tape back to set the scene before the story.

SPIDER'S WEB

Most of the spiders in the barn were quite happy to spin webs and catch flies—except Veronica. She hated spinning. It left her bored and miserable and cross.

'Just another web, Veronica,' said her mother. 'From that beam to the rusty nail.'

'Do I have to?' Veronica moved across the beam and trailed a thread out towards the nail. Up and down, round and round she went, forming a tangled, uneven mess. She was quite dazed and giddy by the end. She sighed. 'I'll never get it right,' she said.

'Happy as usual!' called out a little orange spider from the beam above her.

'Go away,' snapped Veronica, 'or I'll eat you.'

'Not all spiders spin webs.' The orange spider backed away from her slightly. 'I don't. Why do it if you don't want to?'

'I'm the kind that does,' replied Veronica. 'You can't choose what kind of spider you are.'

'Seems to me you're the odd kind.'

Veronica ran towards the spider, who turned and fled. She went back to the corner of her web and sat in the shadows, waiting for a fly to land. Something tugged the web near her foot. She got ready to pounce, but it was one of her brothers.

'Come on,' he said. 'Uncle Byron has something to tell us.'

Veronica followed the other spiders up into the hayloft, where her uncle stood perched on a flowerpot, looking very important. 'This barn is our home,' he began. Veronica could tell by the sound of his voice that this was going to take a long time. 'It has been our home for generations, for hundreds of years. And now—it is to be our home no longer.'

There were gasps of horror from the crowd. 'Yes, dear friends. Our barn is to be pulled down and turned into—holiday flats!'

Veronica felt afraid. It was the only world she had ever known.

'There is only one thing we can do,' continued Uncle Byron. 'We must move to the cattle shed. It is not so pleasant, but there are plenty of flies.'

That night a small army of spiders crossed the yard by the light of the moon. They felt creatures watching them on every side, but they kept going—all except Veronica.

She found herself wandering away from the barns towards the fields. 'What does it matter where I go?' she thought.

The next morning, as it grew light, Veronica woke to the soft munching sound of cows in the field. A soft mist hung over the grass and the hedge where she had been sleeping. She moved to the end of a twig and looked out. There before her was the most wonderful sight she had ever seen—a huge spider's web, sparkling with tiny drops of dew, stretched from the stile to the gatepost. It was perfect, not a tangle or a crossed strand anywhere. It looked strong and fragile and beautiful all at the same time.

'Oh,' she breathed. 'If only I could make webs like that!'

'Why don't you, then?' asked a large, green spider running across the top of the web.

'I can't. I just make a mess of it.'

'Maybe,' said the green spider, 'you've never really wanted to before. It makes all the difference. Go on, try.'

Veronica ran over to the cow shed and up into the roof. The others were already busy with their webs. 'Veronica!' they called. 'Where have you been?'

She didn't reply but got to work. First she made a bridge, then she secured it with some other strands, then she carefully put in some lines to the centre. And finally she began moving outwards, round and round, making a perfect spiral. The strange thing was, she felt happy.

'How did you learn to do that?' asked a voice. It was the little orange spider who'd followed them from the barn.

'I just found I wanted to,' she said. 'I like making webs.'

> **I want your act of kindness to come from your heart.**
> PHILEMON 14

BIBLE REFERENCES

Psalm 37:3–6; Ezekiel 36:24–28; Luke 24:13–33; Philemon 8–18

SERMON POINTERS

★ **Psalm 37:3–6**: How can we do what God wants, and still have our own desires? What are your heart's desires?

★ **Ezekiel 36:24–28**: Why was it necessary for God to give his people new hearts? How does willingness connect with obedience?

★ **Luke 24:13–33**: What change of heart occurred in the two disciples? Why was this significant for them? Do we dismiss the voice of our hearts too easily?

★ **Philemon 8–18**: Why was it important that Philemon was not forced into kindness? Do we try to force people to love others? Does God force us?

QUESTIONS FOR YOUNGER LISTENERS

★ What was wrong with the webs Veronica made?
★ Why did she make them so badly?
★ What happened to change her?
★ Are we willing to do what God wants?
★ How does he help us to be willing?

VISUAL AIDS AND ACTIONS

* Cotton or string
* An open-backed chair

Make a spider's web with cotton or string across the back of a chair.

⁜

THE WISE WOLVES

The wolf cubs rolled and snapped and chased each other round in circles. Wendle, the eldest, dug his tiny teeth into his brother's fur. Barrel yelped and gave up. Wendle chased his sister, Charlie, but she turned and growled at him, her fur standing on end. He paused. Charlie was younger and smaller, but wildly fierce. Wendle backed away and started sniffing the trunk of a tree.

Over the next few months, the cubs grew bigger and stronger. They learned many things about life in the forest, and the rules of belonging to the pack. Then Barrel disappeared. They thought he might have been shot by a hunter or caught in a trap. The pack moved on, roaming the hills, knowing that winter was coming.

Winter taught the wolves about hunger and darkness and cold. It also taught them courage and cunning, as they moved in closer to dangerous places where food could be found, padding silently and swiftly over the snow.

A year went by, and then another. Winter came, a harder winter than before. Then, one day, Barrel returned, limping, part of his foot missing. He'd been living among humans, he said. The other wolves growled, and backed away from him.

Wendle and Charlie began hunting food for Barrel as well. Being lame, he was not fast enough to hunt for himself. The other wolves disapproved. They knew that a weak wolf was no good to the pack— but they also knew it was not wise to quarrel with Wendle and Charlie.

As winter deepened, the wolves grew more and more angry that Barrel was eating food they could have had. One day, they closed in, led by the pack leader. Wendle, Barrel and Charlie stood in a circle, facing outwards, their teeth bared.

'You're putting us all in danger,' said the pack leader. 'Barrel has to leave.' The wolves growled in agreement.

'We need him!' Charlie cried. 'Kill him, and the pack will go hungry.'

'How is this true?' The pack leader did not sound as if he believed it.

It was Wendle who replied. 'Barrel is the one who tells us where to hunt. He finds the tracks and smells the prey long before we do. He is the wisest of us all. And he knows the ways of humans. He knows where they store their food, and where they throw out their rubbish. If we listen to him, there will be enough for us all.'

The wolves began to snarl and mutter, uncertain what to do.

'What about the law?' someone asked. 'Weak animals must die. Wolf law must be obeyed.' There were howls of agreement all around.

'Wolf law must be understood,' cried Wendle. 'You are being stupid. Wolf law doesn't require you to be stupid.'

The other wolf stepped forward, his head lowered dangerously. Charlie growled and then shot forward and seized him by the ear. He turned on her. The pack leader barked sharply, and they all stood still.

'Wendle is right,' he said. 'The pack is stronger if Barrel is with us. Let him stay.'

Wendle relaxed. The wolves began to move away, grumbling.

'You have also grown wise,' said the pack leader to Wendle. 'I can see we will have a new leader one day.' And he went over to talk to Barrel about the ways of humans and where they store their food.

> **Don't be stupid. Instead, find out what the Lord wants you to do.** EPHESIANS 5:17

BIBLE REFERENCES

Proverbs 4:10–13; Luke 2:40; Ephesians 5:8–20; James 1:2–8

SERMON POINTERS

⋆ **Proverbs 4:10–13:** Do we think of God's way as 'the way that makes sense'? What are the consequences of going the right way?

⋆ **Luke 2:40:** Do we imagine Jesus needing to become wise? How might he have learnt? How can we help our young people to grow in wisdom?

⋆ **Ephesians 5:8–20:** What does Paul mean by 'the dark' and 'evil times'? How are we to avoid being foolish? Do we strive to be people of good sense?

⋆ **James 1:2–8:** What does James see as the benefit of hardship? How are wisdom and maturity to be gained?

QUESTIONS FOR YOUNGER LISTENERS

⋆ What was the law the wolves were talking about?

⋆ Why did the other wolves want Barrel to go?

⋆ Why did the pack leader agree that he could stay?

⋆ How can we learn to make wise choices?

⋆ How does God help us make good choices?

VISUAL AIDS AND ACTIONS

⋆ A paper full moon

⋆ A dark paper circle, slightly larger, to eclipse the moon

Ask the children what wolves do at full moon. If they would like to, let them demonstrate wolves howling as you reveal the full moon.

THE CLOWN AND
THE ELEPHANT

Gemma loved to make people laugh. She enjoyed the sound of their laughter so much that it made her do handsprings—on the inside as well as the outside. And people did laugh at her, because Gemma was a clown in the circus.

But Gemma had a secret, and there was nothing funny about it. Gemma was not her real name. Her real name was quite different and hard to pronounce.

Gemma came from a country where the government was dangerous and violent, and she had got into trouble with them. She was afraid they would arrest her and treat her badly, so she had run away. She had joined the circus because it kept on travelling, and she felt safe while she was moving from place to place.

But one day Gemma saw two men coming out of her caravan, and she knew they were looking for her. She was sure they had been sent by her government to arrest her and take her back, and suddenly she was very frightened indeed.

Gemma needed somewhere to hide, and she had to act fast. But where could she go and whom could she trust? She thought about the ringmaster. No, he was too fond of a pint of beer, and too fond of talking.

The trapeze artists? Could she trust them? No, they were jealous that she could swing through the air so easily and clown at the same time. She would need to find someone kind, someone honest, someone brave. All her friends in the circus were fun to be with, but she didn't know what they would do if they knew about her past.

Gemma could see the two men in the distance talking to one of the technicians, whose job it was to put up the big tent and make sure the ropes were safe. She crept back a few steps and found herself at one of the entrances to the circus ring. Inside, a young boy was working with one of the elephants, training him to do his act.

She knew the boy slightly—he was quiet and a bit shy, but she also knew that when he did speak, he said what he meant. And if he ever promised to do something, he always did it. His name was Carlo, and he'd been with the circus about a year.

'Easy, Bubble, easy. Right foot, right foot. Good boy!' Carlo was speaking to Bubble the elephant in such a firm, friendly way that Gemma felt sure she could trust him.

'Carlo,' she said, entering the ring. 'Carlo, I need your help.'

A few moments passed and then the two men entered the big tent. They watched the young man teaching the elephant to count to ten. Bubble was sitting on a large wooden block, his back legs crossed, a pair of huge green spectacles on his trunk. The men smiled briefly and then carried on searching the tent.

'No one here, come on,' said one. 'She's not here.'

'She never was,' said the other. 'It's another false trail.'

And they left.

Bubble the elephant stood up and, at a command from Carlo, lifted the sturdy wooden block clean into the air. Gemma climbed out and dusted herself down.

'You OK?' asked Carlo.

'I am now. Carlo, thank you. I owe you my life.' There was a pause, and then Gemma laughed. 'You know, that's the funniest thing that's ever happened to me. I've been sat on by an elephant. And the worst thing is, I can't tell anyone!'

> **God can be trusted, and so can I.** 2 CORINTHIANS 1:18

BIBLE REFERENCES

Psalm 71:5–6; Proverbs 11:13; John 2:23–25;
2 Corinthians 1:12–22

SERMON POINTERS

✶ **Psalm 71:5–6**: The psalmist can say that God has proved reliable in his own life. Can we say the same?

✶ **Proverbs 11:13**: Do we know how to treasure confidences? Or is it too easy to 'share' someone else's story? Whom can you trust with a confidence?

✶ **John 2:23–25**: Why did Jesus not trust the people in Jerusalem? Can we tell whom to trust?

✶ **2 Corinthians 1:12–22**: How does Paul defend his trustworthiness to the Corinthian church? How does he see trustworthiness relating to the Christian life?

QUESTIONS FOR YOUNGER LISTENERS

✶ Why did Gemma trust Carlo?
✶ What makes us able to trust someone?
✶ Is there someone you know you can trust?
✶ Can people trust you?
✶ Do you think Jesus can be trusted? Why?

VISUAL AIDS AND ACTIONS

✶ A clown mask or a red nose

Children can try on the clown mask. Talk about why clowns wear masks or make-up.

THE BAMBOO HOUSE

'Bricks are best!' said the brick house, not for the first time. 'Bricks are best. Oh, you can build with wood or metal, or sticks or stones, or even mud and straw. But bricks last. Bricks stand firm. Bricks can be trusted!'

His windows gleamed in the sun in a satisfied way. They were very pleased to be part of a brick house. He was a large house as well, the largest in town. There were other brick houses standing nearby, and they listened to his words and agreed with him.

'Wood is for garden sheds,' the brick house went on, 'and mud is for pig sties. But if you want to build a house, bricks are best.'

He'd said it before, but today he was saying it loudly and often, because down the other end of the town a very poor family had arrived. They were building their house out of bamboo sticks. They were tying the bamboo together with twine, and they'd already built the floor standing on legs above the ground. By the end of the week the house was finished, and its roof was made of huge leaves sewn together.

There were several children in the family and they wandered about the streets, staring up at the brick houses as if they had never seen anything like them before.

'I tell you,' said the big house to his neighbours. 'Bricks are best. Bricks stand firm.'

The other houses, even the wooden ones, repeated his words right down the street until someone passed them on to the bamboo sticks. The bamboo house felt a little ashamed. 'I do wobble a bit,' she said.

Her words were repeated back up the street to the big house, who laughed loudly. 'See! Can't trust a house that's weak and wobbly.'

The bamboo house looked down at her family sadly. 'I'm all they've got,' she said. 'I do my best.'

Soon the children had made friends in the town and had begun to go to a little school.

The school was in a wooden cabin. 'Don't listen to that brick house,' the wooden cabin said to the bamboo, who was his neighbour. 'He's not as strong as he thinks.'

One day, a terrible thing happened. Several miles away there was an earthquake, and the little town was shaken by earth tremors. Some of the badly built houses fell down. People ran about shouting for help. Many ran into the street because they did not trust the buildings. But the poor family all ran home and climbed up into their bamboo house. There was a loud crack and a crash, and then the earthquake was over.

The houses left standing began to whisper together. The wooden cabin called to the bamboo house, 'I'm a bit broken. They'll have to repair me. I'm glad there were no children here when it happened. Are you all right?'

'Yes, I'm fine,' said the bamboo house. 'A bit wobbly, though, as usual.'

'That's why you're still there,' said the cabin. 'You could bend and move with the earthquake. But I hear that the big house in the centre of town has broken in half. They'll have to pull it down. Those brick houses that won't bend—you can't trust them.'

So the brick house came down. The owners moved away and the land was sold. And in its place some new houses were built, made of bamboo. They didn't look very strong but people bought them because they knew they could be trusted.

> **He chose the weak things of this world to put the powerful to shame.** 1 CORINTHIANS 1:27

BIBLE REFERENCES

Psalm 20:7–8; Mark 10:17–27; 1 Corinthians 1:18–31;
2 Corinthians 12:8–10

SERMON POINTERS

⭐ **Psalm 20:7–8**: What is the equivalent in our lives of chariots and horses?

⭐ **Mark 10:17–27**: In what way was this young man righteous? And in what way did he fail? What can we learn from him?

⭐ **1 Corinthians 1:18–31**: What insight does this give us about true value judgments? How can we apply this to our church communities?

⭐ **2 Corinthians 12:8–10**: What is our true strength, and where does it come from? In what way was Jesus weak?

QUESTIONS FOR YOUNGER LISTENERS

⭐ What was the brick house boasting about?

⭐ When the earthquake came, what happened to him?

⭐ Why was the bamboo house better?

⭐ What different things do people trust in today?

⭐ The Bible tells us to put our trust in God. How can we do that?

VISUAL AIDS AND ACTIONS

⭐ Sheets of newspaper

Give each child a sheet of newspaper to tear in half. Ask them if newspaper is weak or strong. Give them a second sheet, tell them to fold it in half seven times, and see if they can still tear it.

+++

THE EAGLE WHO
WOULDN'T FLY

Baby Eagle looked over the edge of the nest and closed his eyes. 'I'm not leaving!' he said, and he clung to the side of the nest. 'I'm not the flying sort.'

'Don't be silly,' said his mother. 'Of course you are. Come on, jump.'

Baby Eagle shrank back in the nest. 'I'd rather do it tomorrow. I've got a funny tummy.'

'All your brothers and sisters can fly,' sighed his mother.

'Yes, I know,' Baby Eagle agreed. 'But I have different skills. I can squawk in three languages.'

His mother flapped her huge wings and glided down the side of the mountain. Baby Eagle looked up into the great blue sky and down towards the vast blue sea, and he shuddered. 'If only I could be sure,' he thought. 'I'll wait till my wings are bigger.'

The branch shook as his father landed near the nest. 'Son,' he said, 'do you *want* to fly?'

Baby Eagle put his head on one side. 'Now you mention it, Dad, there's a lot to be said for seeing the world from a nest.'

His father looked at him steadily. 'If you want to fly, you have to trust me.'

Baby Eagle gulped. 'Trust you?'

'Yes. When you jump, I'll be flying very close to you. If there's any danger of you falling, I'll fly underneath and catch you.'

Baby Eagle thought of his father's outstretched wings, over two metres across. He thought of the way his father could turn in the air like an acrobat, could soar and dive and streak down to earth to catch his prey. And he thought it would be very safe in the air if his father was nearby to help him.

'Think about it, son,' said his father quietly and flew away.

Baby Eagle began to fret. He knew that the nest would soon be too small for him. He knew that his parents couldn't feed him for the rest of his life. He knew that deep down he wanted to fly, more than anything. Baby Eagle struggled up on to the rim of the nest and clutched it tightly with his talons. The nest was swaying slightly in the wind. He could see his father circling below, and his mother arriving with food in her beak.

'If only I could trust him,' he thought sadly.

Then suddenly a great push from his mother sent him screeching into the air. He felt the wind rushing through his feathers and his wings automatically stretch out. And there was his father, just beneath him, almost touching him, keeping close.

'That's right, son,' he called. 'Move your feathers, like this, so you can turn in the air.'

'I'm flying, I'm flying!' cried Baby Eagle. 'I can do it!'

Clumsily, he flapped his way back to the nest and fell in. 'That was brilliant!' he squawked. 'Let's do it again!'

'Have some food first,' said his mother, and he realized how hungry he was.

'You pushed me,' Baby Eagle accused her when he'd finished eating.

His mother preened herself. 'We pushed all your brothers and sisters. They'd never have jumped otherwise.'

'Dad told me he'd be there,' said Baby Eagle, 'but I didn't believe him.'

'No, but I did,' said his mother.

'Come on!' Jesus said. MATTHEW 14:29

BIBLE REFERENCES

Deuteronomy 32:11; Isaiah 43:1–2; Matthew 14:22–33; James 2:14–26

SERMON POINTERS

★ **Deuteronomy 32:11:** What do we learn from this verse about God's relationship with his people?

★ **Isaiah 43:1–2:** Is this the guarantee of a troublefree life? Or the promise of God's presence in all circumstances? Do you have your own stories of the truth of this verse?

★ **Matthew 14:22–33:** How did Jesus respond to Peter in this story? What might God be asking us to step out and do in our own lives?

★ **James 2:14–26:** What examples does James give of faith in action? How can we be sure that our faith is alive?

QUESTIONS FOR YOUNGER LISTENERS

★ Why didn't Baby Eagle want to leave the nest?

★ What did he learn in the end?

★ How did you feel when you learnt to swim or ride a bicycle?

★ What did Jesus ask his disciples to do, and how did he help them?

★ If we follow Jesus, how will he help us?

VISUAL AIDS AND ACTIONS

Invite an older child to fall backwards while a responsible adult catches him or her.

THE KING'S PROMISE

One winter's night, two men sat by the fireside warming themselves in front of the flames. One was a rich merchant. The other, whose house they were in, was the local doctor. The doctor was not a poor man, but his work did not bring in much money.

'I have to say, I've done well for myself,' said the merchant. 'If I see something I like, I buy it. But you, you're so busy helping people for nothing, you'll never be a rich man.'

The doctor stared into the fire for a few moments. 'You're wrong,' he said quietly. 'I believe I'm richer than you.'

'Are you?' The merchant looked surprised. 'I see no sign of it. Secret treasure, perhaps?'

'In a way.' The doctor crossed to the mantelpiece and reached down a small wooden box. He lifted the lid and took out a gold ring decorated with a single jewel.

'It is beautiful,' said the merchant. 'I will buy it from you if you will name a price.'

The doctor shook his head. 'This ring is worth more than you could ever afford.'

And then he told his story. A young boy, travelling with his family, had been brought to the house in a high fever. The doctor had given the boy care and medicine and he had recovered. He could tell that his guests were important people, but only as they were leaving did he discover that the boy was the king's youngest son. Some days later, a messenger arrived from the king. The messenger gave the doctor a gold ring and told him it was a sign that the king would always be his friend.

'So you see,' ended the doctor, 'this ring is a promise of friendship —a king's friendship. And it is very precious.'

'If I were you,' said the merchant, 'I'd sell the ring and buy something of real value. Kings are not always to be trusted.'

'True,' the doctor agreed. 'But I believe he is a man of his word.'

As hard as he tried, the merchant could not persuade the doctor to sell his ring. But that night the doctor began to wonder if he was right. Surely, a promise to a poor doctor meant nothing. Better to sell the ring and live in comfort. The next day he took the ring from its box and set out to find a jeweller. He began to dream of all the things he would buy.

But a terrible shock awaited him. When the jeweller looked at the ring, he saw a tiny crown stamped inside, and he knew that it belonged to the king. 'The doctor must have stolen it,' he thought. Within minutes, the doctor had been arrested and thrown into jail. He could persuade no one that he was the king's friend. 'Ask the king,' he pleaded. 'Take the ring and ask him!'

'If it's so precious to you, why sell it?' said the jailer. 'Fine friend you are.'

Days went by, and then one morning the doctor looked up through the bars to see the king's messenger talking to the jailer. The jailer came over and unlocked the door.

'Seems you were telling the truth,' he said.

The doctor took the ring from the jailer, and went over to the king's messenger. 'Here is the ring,' he said. 'I suppose the king will want it back now.'

'You are wrong,' replied the messenger. 'The king has given his promise. He will not take it back. He will always be your friend.'

'Then tell him,' said the doctor, 'that I make him a promise. I shall never try to sell this ring again. It is the most precious thing I have.'

And the doctor kept his word.

> **God never tells a lie!** TITUS 1:2

BIBLE REFERENCES

1 Kings 8:22–26; Luke 2:25–32; Galatians 3:12–29; Titus 1:1–3

SERMON POINTERS

★ **1 Kings 8:22–26**: How has God fulfilled his promises to David? What can we learn about God's nature from these verses?

★ **Luke 2:25–32**: What promise of God did Simeon see fulfilled? What promises has God made to you that have been fulfilled?

★ **Galatians 3:12–29**: What are the different promises found in these verses? What is the significance of faith in receiving God's promises?

★ **Titus 1:1–3**: What is the message that God gave to Paul? What message do we announce? How can we receive the promise of eternal life?

QUESTIONS FOR YOUNGER LISTENERS

★ What was so precious about the doctor's ring?

★ Why did the doctor decide to sell it?

★ How did the king keep his promise?

★ Do we trust God to keep his promises?

★ What promises did Jesus make to his disciples?

VISUAL AIDS AND ACTIONS

★ A wedding or engagement ring

★ A five-pound note

★ Tickets

★ Party invitation

★ Passport

Talk about the different promises attached to these objects.

❖

THE TELESCOPE

Mr Focus kept a shop just off the high street. It was a small shop, crammed with things to buy. He sold telescopes for seeing the stars, binoculars for birdwatching, microscopes so that you could see the tiniest creatures living, and magnifying glasses to read the smallest print. Everything he sold helped you to see things more clearly.

But there was one thing Mr Focus did not sell. He did not sell anything that could see into the future—and Mr Focus worried about the future a lot. He worried about the planet, and whether it would run out of oil and water and trees. He worried about his health, and about wars and diseases. And he worried about money. It made him quite selfish, and he never missed the chance to sell something for the highest price he could get.

Every Saturday morning, a young boy came into the shop to look around. He never bought anything, he just looked. One day, Mr Focus asked him what he wanted.

'I'm saving up,' said the boy.

'What are you saving up *for*?' snapped Mr Focus.

'A telescope,' said the boy.

Now Mr Focus sold lots of telescopes. Some were very small and were really no more than toys. Others were for watching birds and animals. The biggest and most powerful were for looking at the stars, and they came with a computer programme that told you the names of all the stars for every night of the year.

'Well, you'd better hurry,' grumbled Mr Focus. 'I'm putting the prices up soon.'

For a long time the boy didn't return to the shop, and Mr Focus forgot about him. As the days passed, Mr Focus became ill. It was because he worried so much. The stock on his shelves began to run down, and he didn't bother to replace it. The shop became tatty and dusty, and fewer and fewer people came in to buy anything.

But Mr Focus was too frightened to put his prices down, in case he needed the money.

Then, one day, as Mr Focus sat in the corner of his dusty shop, the door opened and in walked the young boy.

'I've come to buy the telescope,' he said. 'I've saved up.'

'Which one do you want?' asked Mr Focus gloomily.

'The one where you can see the stars.'

Mr Focus raised his head. 'Why do you want to look at the stars?'

The boy went over to a glass case and peered inside. 'I need to know about them,' he explained. 'I'm going to be an astronaut one day.'

He seemed so certain about it that Mr Focus felt angry. 'Oh, are you?' he said. 'And suppose the world blows up tomorrow? Suppose you change your mind? An astronaut, indeed!'

The boy thought for a while, and then he replied, 'If I do nothing, I'll never be one.'

The boy's words had a strange effect on Mr Focus. He began to think. Why was he always worrying about what *might* happen in the future? It was now that he needed to think about. Now was the time to make choices. And this young boy had got it right. He was aiming for the stars but he was living for today.

For the first time in many years, Mr Focus felt light-hearted and generous. He wrapped up the biggest telescope in his shop and gave it to the boy. 'Half-price,' he said, and he smiled.

> **'Don't worry about tomorrow.'** MATTHEW 6:34

BIBLE REFERENCES

Job 19:23–27; Matthew 6:25–34; Luke 12:16–21; 1 Peter 1:3–9

SERMON POINTERS

* **Job 19:23–27:** What is the hope that Job has for the future? What is the basis for his hope, and can we share it?
* **Matthew 6:25–34:** Are we to abandon all plans and ambitions? What is the central point of Jesus' teaching in these verses? How can we apply this to our busy, demanding lives?
* **Luke 12:16–21:** What was the rich man's attitude to the present and the future? What had he overlooked? Do we make the same mistake?
* **1 Peter 1:3–9:** How can we be confident that our future is secure? What references do these verses make to faith?

QUESTIONS FOR YOUNGER LISTENERS

* What did Mr Focus worry about and what sort of person did it make him?
* Why did the young boy want to buy a telescope?
* Why did Mr Focus sell him the telescope at half-price?
* What did Mr Focus learn about the future?
* Why did Jesus tell his disciples not to worry about the future?

VISUAL AIDS AND ACTIONS

* Telescope
* Binoculars
* Microscope
* Magnifying glass

Ask the children what each instrument is for.

❖

THE WOODCUTTER'S GIFTS

Once there was a poor woodcutter called Piers, who lived in the
forest with his son Jon. Each day, the woodcutter would take his axe
and chop logs to sell in the market. It was hard work and he made
little money. Jon helped his father by roping the logs together so that
they could be dragged over the ground. 'This is horses' work!'
grumbled Piers as he took hold of the rope, and he raised his voice
to the trees. 'I wish I had a horse!'

The next morning, Jon called his father to the window. There,
tethered to the gatepost, was a great chestnut mare. Piers opened his
eyes in astonishment and ran down the path. 'The wood folk!' he
said. 'The fairies! They heard my prayers!'

Jon looked about on the ground and saw a set of footprints
leading to a path in the woods. 'Look, Dad!' he said. 'Footsteps.' But
Piers was too busy admiring the horse to listen.

That day, they worked hard and the horse easily pulled the logs
along the ground to the cottage. Soon they had a great pile of wood.
'I wish I had a cart to go with the horse,' called Piers loudly. 'Then I
could carry all these logs to market.'

The next morning, there stood a wooden cart, with high spoked
wheels and steep sides. Piers laughed. 'See, they heard my prayers!'
But Jon again saw the footprints, and again his father was too busy
trying out the cart to listen.

That day, as they chopped logs in the wood, Piers began to make
plans. He could soon make a bit of money and send Jon to school.
He could even sell the horse if he didn't have enough. Jon was a
bright boy and would do well. As they finished loading the cart, Piers
lifted his head and shouted, 'I wish I had a bag of gold!' Then he
winked at Jon. 'No harm trying, is there?'

The next morning, on the doorstep were three gold pieces tied up
in a roll of cloth. It was more money than Piers had ever had in his
life. 'Not bad,' he said. 'But I hoped it would be more.'

Jon saw the footprints again. 'Dad,' he said firmly. 'I'm going to follow these footprints. Someone keeps giving us things. Don't you want to know who it is?'

Piers sighed. 'You're right, son. It's time we found out. Even if everything has to go back.'

They started following the prints along the pathway, and found themselves going deeper and deeper into the woods. The trees grew closer together and thick brambles began to make walking difficult. They wondered if they were lost. But then Jon saw a piece of cloth caught on a bramble and knew that someone had walked that way.

At last they came to a clearing and there was a small stone house, the front door standing open. 'Is anyone there?' called Piers.

A man came out, a man who was smiling and holding out his arms. 'Don't you know me, Piers?' he said.

'Josh! My brother Josh! After all these years! Back from your travels at last.'

'I've come back with a bit of money, Piers—and I'm willing to share it with you and your boy.'

The two brothers hugged each other. 'I thought I'd never see you again,' said Piers. 'We had a bad quarrel, didn't we?'

'That's over now,' said Josh. 'Let's have a look at my nephew, then.'

Piers smiled. 'It's because of him that I found you. He saw the footprints. He wanted to find out who was giving to us. I was only thinking about the gifts.'

'I'm glad you came looking,' said Josh to his nephew.

'So am I,' said Jon. 'You're the best gift of all.'

Every good and perfect gift comes down from the Father.
JAMES 1:17

BIBLE REFERENCES

Hosea 2:2–8; John 6:22–29; James 1:12–18; 1 John 3:19–24

SERMON POINTERS

* **Hosea 2:2–8**: How is Israel depicted in these verses? What mistakes did the people make?
* **John 6:22–29**: What is the point that Jesus is making? How might we seek God for the wrong reasons? What is the work we're being asked to do?
* **James 1:12–18**: What are the gifts that James has in mind? How do they all relate to God? What is the outcome that God intends?
* **1 John 3:19–24**: What do we learn that God wants of us? What will he do for us? What do we want of him?

QUESTIONS FOR YOUNGER LISTENERS

* Who did Piers think had brought the gifts?
* Did he really care who gave them to him?
* Why did Jon want to follow the footprints?
* Can you think of something God has given you?
* What does God want from us?

VISUAL AIDS AND ACTIONS

* Various wrapped objects and paper footprints

Lay a trail of wrapped objects and paper footprints for the children to follow, ending up at yourself or someone else.

⁘

THE SPRING

Once there was a shepherd who lived in a hut in the mountains. Every day he would walk the hills with his sheep until he'd found them good pasture. At night he'd go back to his hut. It was a hard life and a lonely one, and sometimes he longed for company.

Near the hut was a hot spring that flowed out of the mountainside and ran over the stones. Every evening the shepherd would take off his heavy boots, peel off his smelly socks and bathe his feet in the warm water.

'Aaaaah!' he'd sigh. 'That's the stuff!'

One evening, as he sat with his feet in the small stream, he had an idea. What if he put some of the water in a bottle and sold it in the market? He'd make a bit of money.

People would buy anything if it was in a bottle.

So the shepherd collected together some old jars and bottles from the rubbish heap, washed them out and filled them with spring water. Then he took his wheelbarrow and went to market.

The market was noisy and bustling and he was surrounded by traders, calling out all that they had to sell. He began shouting, 'Buy a bottle of spring water. Hot spring water for tired feet. Puts the spring back in your legs!'

'I could do with some of that,' said a woman to her friends. She paid a few coins and the shepherd gave her a bottle. The woman unscrewed the lid and took a mouthful.

'Huh!' she said. 'It's just water. What's special about that? I want my money back!'

A farmer came along and picked up one of the jars. 'Thought you said it was hot spring water. Feels cold to me. Where'd you get it?'

Another man examined the bottles carefully. 'Hmm… cloudy,' he said. 'Mineral deposits, I suppose. Very clever. Makes it look genuine.'

'It is genuine!' cried the shepherd. 'You can see for yourself. Up the sheep track, near the shepherd's hut!'

By the end of the day, nobody had bought a single bottle. The shepherd felt very disappointed. He packed up his wheelbarrow and headed for the road. That evening, he sat by the spring feeling very miserable and lonely, but as usual the warm water bathed his feet and made him feel better.

The next day, one of the traders from the market walked up the track to the hut.

'Show me this spring,' he said. 'Let's see if it's as good as you say.' He took off his boots and dipped his feet into the stream. 'Ah, it's great!' he cried. 'Worth the climb!'

Soon, people were coming up the mountain regularly to bathe their feet. Sometimes the shepherd gave them bread and cheese and a cup of tea. Sometimes they brought him cake or a basket of fruit.

The shepherd carried on looking after his sheep and walking over the hills, but he was no longer lonely. There was always someone visiting the spring for him to talk to.

Some were visitors from other lands, and they had many stories to tell. Others were local folk, and they became his friends.

The shepherd smiled as he thought of the way he'd tried to bottle the water and sell it—and how much more he'd gained by simply telling people where it could be found.

> **'If you are thirsty, come to me and drink!'** JOHN 7:37

BIBLE REFERENCES

Jeremiah 2:9–13; John 4:3–15; John 7:37–39; Revelation 22:17

SERMON POINTERS

* **Jeremiah 2:9–13** What were the leaking and cracked pits that Jeremiah refers to? What might they be in our lives?
* **John 4:3–15** How is the woman's interest engaged? Does she appreciate what she is asking for at this stage? How can we nurture people who are beginning to show interest in Jesus?
* **John 7:37–39** How might people be thirsty in our society? How can we explain to them the invitation of Jesus?
* **Revelation 22:17** How are we to share in the invitation? In the receiving? In the giving?

QUESTIONS FOR YOUNGER LISTENERS

* What was so good about the spring water in the mountains?
* Why did the shepherd try to bottle it?
* What did he learn was a better idea?
* What did Jesus say about life-giving water?
* What did he invite people to do?

VISUAL AIDS AND ACTIONS

* A bottle of spring water

Ask the children why water is so important.

THE ANT AND THE BICYCLE

Sally could hear her brother calling for help. Paul was trying to get his bicycle over the stile, but he was too small to lift it by himself. Sally was lying in the sun by the riverbank, and she couldn't be bothered to help anyone. 'Leave it, Paul,' she called. 'No one's going to steal a kid's bike.'

'Please, Sally, it's heavy.'

'You shouldn't have come, then.'

Sally picked a blade of grass and began to chew. She could hear her brother tugging and whimpering as he tried to lift the bike. She hoped he'd give up and go home. Small brothers were just a nuisance most of the time. Her brother called again. 'Sally, the bike's stuck.' Paul had managed to wedge the handlebars under the stile and jam the back mudguard into the bushes.

'I'm busy.' Sally stared into the tangled world of grass and leaves inches from her face. She noticed an ant dragging a single leaf along. The ant pulled, and the leaf moved slowly forward, then stuck fast between a stone and a mound of earth. The ant ran round, waving its antennae, trying to pull the leaf free. Sally was wondering whether to help the ant or to squash it when it turned and ran off through the grass.

'You have to help me,' cried Paul.

'Why?' said Sally.

'You're my sister.'

Sally watched as another ant joined the first. They stood waving their antennae for a few moments, and then both ants went back to the leaf. Sally didn't know that ants could talk to each other. One of them climbed on to the mound of earth while the other pulled the leaf from the front. The leaf rose slightly into the air and tipped over the stone, and together the two ants tugged it forward across the ground.

'They've done it!' thought Sally. 'Wow! That's so clever!'

A small foot landed near the ants. 'Careful!' she cried angrily. 'You nearly trod on them.' Paul sat down next to his sister and threw a stone into the river. Sally watched the ants come to a hole in the ground, then reverse down into the hole taking the leaf with them. After they had gone, the grass seemed to go very still.

Sally wondered what it was like being an ant. She didn't know if ants really talked to each other, but the second one had been willing to help. Perhaps the first one had begged and begged. Perhaps they were friends. She was pleased they had managed to get the leaf home.

'Where's your bike?' she said.

'I told you, it's stuck.' Paul sounded a bit tearful.

'Come on, we'll get it.'

Paul grinned and ran back to the hedge. Sally pushed and Paul pulled, and the bike was soon free. She lifted it over the stile.

'Race you to that bush!' shouted Paul, pedalling fast along the path. Sally picked her own bike up off the grass and followed him.

Never stop praying, especially for others. EPHESIANS 6:18

BIBLE REFERENCES

1 Samuel 1:1–18; Luke 18:1–8; Acts 1:14; Ephesians 6:18–20

SERMON POINTERS

* ✶ **1 Samuel 1:1–18:** What state was Hannah in when she prayed? What made her go on praying? How can we know when to persevere and when to accept?
* ✶ **Luke 18:1–8:** What is meant to be the lesson of these verses? Will God give us anything if we ask enough times? What prompts God to answer us?

* **Acts 1:14**: What is the significance of this verse at the beginning of Acts? How can we ensure that our church community is a praying community?
* **Ephesians 6:18–20**: Why is prayer emphasized here by Paul? What are the important points he makes? What is he acknowledging about his own ministry?

QUESTIONS FOR YOUNGER LISTENERS

* Why didn't Sally help Paul?
* What did she learn from watching the ants?
* Why did she help Paul in the end?
* What does the Bible tell us about how often we should pray?
* Will God hear us because we pray a lot or because he loves us?

VISUAL AIDS AND ACTIONS

* Make a prayer board or a prayer card.

Ask the children for items to put on the board or card, to remind them to go on praying for people.

THE FISH'S TALE

Finny the fish swam closer to the cave. The noise around him was deafening. Several multi-coloured fish were gliding to and fro, while the oysters clapped and cheered and asked for autographs. One beautiful fish with long tail-fins was being interviewed by an eel.

'Yes, I've known Ahab the octopus for years. I've worked in all his films. I'm very confident of a part in his next production. We talk several times a week, you know.'

'Do you?' asked the eel. 'You talk to him in person?'

The fish opened her large yellow eyes wide. 'Of course,' she bubbled.

Finny darted forward between the rows of oysters and moved towards the mouth of the cave. 'And where are you going?' asked a lobster, with claws snapping.

'I've come to see Ahab,' said Finny timidly.

'Not you,' sneered the lobster. 'Why should he want to see you?'

Finny hesitated and drew back. He had turned to swim away when he saw a young octopus move out from under a stone nearby. 'Come here,' whispered the octopus. 'What are you doing here?'

'I wanted to see Ahab,' said Finny.

'Why?'

Finny didn't know what to say next. He wanted to explain how wonderful Ahab's films were, how they'd changed his life. But he knew it would sound feeble. Then some deep wish bubbled up inside him and burst into words: '*I* want to make films!' He felt as if the young octopus now knew everything about him.

A group of shining silver fish with blue streaks along their sides swam out of the cave. 'Wonderful time,' they told the eel. 'Ahab is so charming, so talented.'

'Did he promise you a job in his next film?' asked the eel.

'Oh, we can't tell you that. Let's just say, we got on extremely well.' The fish moved on to mingle with the crowds.

Finny looked disappointed. 'Don't worry about them,' said his new friend. 'They're always showing off. They don't impress my dad much, and they don't impress me.'

Finny opened his eyes in amazement. 'Your dad?'

'Yes. I'm his son. I can teach you if you like. My dad's taught me everything.'

Finny couldn't believe it. 'Oh, that would be great,' he said. 'Thank you.'

'I warn you, though,' said the octopus, 'it won't be easy. And if you go round boasting about it, you won't learn well.'

'I'll try to remember.' Finny had a sudden thought. 'Do they know who you are?'

The octopus shrugged. 'Some of them,' he said. 'But some of them don't care. They're too busy pretending to be my dad's friends. They don't really know him. You must meet him one day. He'll like you.'

Finny felt bubbles of excitement rush through him, and he swam round in circles just for sheer joy. 'I'll see you tomorrow,' he said, and shot away through the clear water to find his friends and tell them all that had happened.

If you want to boast, then boast about the Lord.

2 CORINTHIANS 10:17

BIBLE REFERENCES

Isaiah 37:9–20; Matthew 6:5–8; Luke 18:9–14;
2 Corinthians 10:7–18

SERMON POINTERS

* **Isaiah 37:9–20**: What boast did the king of Assyria make to Hezekiah? How did Hezekiah show humility in his response? What did he believe about God?
* **Matthew 6:5–8**: What different approaches to God in prayer are described here by Jesus? How does Jesus emphasize the relational aspect of prayer?
* **Luke 18:9–14**: Was the Pharisee's prayer a sincere one? Why was it not pleasing to God? Are we ever inclined to boast when we pray?
* **2 Corinthians 10:7–18**: How have the Corinthians been viewing different Christian leaders? Do we veer towards those who outwardly impress? What is Paul's response?

QUESTIONS FOR YOUNGER LISTENERS

* What were all the fish doing outside the cave?
* Why were they showing off?
* What did Finny learn from the young octopus?
* What did Jesus say about people who showed off when they prayed to God?
* What did he tell us we should do when we pray?

VISUAL AIDS AND ACTIONS

* An autograph book

Ask the children what famous autographs they have collected or would like to collect.

THE TRAVELLING WEASELS

This is the story of three weasels called Arthur, Tuppenny and Pop. They used to travel from town to town, where they would dance and play music and make money from the crowds who came to watch them.

One day, they arrived on the edge of a town and had to cross a bridge made of sticks and rope stretched over the river. Halfway across, Arthur noticed a squirrel on the far bank, chewing through the rope. 'Hey, stop!' he cried. 'You'll kill us!'

The squirrel took no notice. Arthur ran forward and grabbed the squirrel's tail, but he kept on gnawing at the rope.

'Run!' cried Pop, and he and Tuppenny turned to get off the bridge. But it was too late. The rope snapped and they tumbled down through the air into the river. Arthur fell backwards, still holding on to the squirrel, and they both plunged into the water.

Tuppenny and Pop went round and round and down and down, their paws waving, trying to swim. A sleek, dark shape glided close and pulled them up to the surface.

They crawled out on to the bank and looked up into the broad face of an otter.

'Are you all right now?' he asked.

'Arthur's missing,' said Pop. 'There's one more.'

'Two more!' said Tuppenny. 'There's a squirrel.'

'Forget the squirrel,' growled Pop.

'No, no,' cried Tuppenny. 'You can't forget him. He's in the water somewhere. Please look for him.'

The otter disappeared. Pop turned on Tuppenny angrily. 'That squirrel tried to drown us! How can you want the otter to save him?'

Tuppenny wrinkled her nose. 'I know. It's horrible—a horrible thing to wish anyone to drown. That's why I can't wish it on the squirrel.'

They stood staring into the water, trying to see the otter. At last he returned, dragging a very soggy squirrel, and pulled him out on to the bank. He whispered a few words in the squirrel's ear, and then went back into the water.

'If Arthur drowns,' said Pop in a dangerous voice, 'I shall push that squirrel back in.'

'There he is!' shouted Tuppenny. Soon, Arthur lay on the bank at their feet, moaning that he felt sick.

'He's alive,' said Pop. 'Thank you, Otter, thank you.'

Tuppenny looked over at the squirrel. 'And thank you for... him,' she added quietly.

'I don't like to see anyone drown,' said the otter. 'Take care of each other.'

The weasels shook themselves dry and gathered round the squirrel, who was lying with his face in his paws. 'Sit up,' said Pop. 'You're all right. The otter saved you.'

'Why did you bite through the rope?' asked Arthur.

The squirrel explained. 'I play the saxophone every night in the park. It's hard making enough money to live. If you'd come into town, there'd have been less of a crowd for me.'

The weasels were thoughtful. They knew what it was to be hungry on a cold night when funds were low.

'What did the otter say to you?' asked Tuppenny.

'He said... I had done a terrible thing. And next time he might not be able to save me.'

'I've an idea,' said Arthur. 'We'll go to the park with you. You'll get a bigger crowd and we can split the profits.'

The squirrel climbed back up the bank with the weasels and together they set off for the town. From among the reeds that grew alongside the riverbank, the bright eyes of the otter watched them go.

'I tell you to love your enemies and pray for anyone who ill-treats you.' MATTHEW 5:44

BIBLE REFERENCES

Job 42:7–9; Matthew 5:43–48; Philippians 3:17–21;
1 Timothy 2:1–6

SERMON POINTERS

* **Job 42:7–9**: How does God show himself to be both judge and saviour? What would Job have learnt from his role?
* **Matthew 5:43–48**: What are the qualities of God's love? Is it possible for us to be like him? How can we help each other in this?
* **Philippians 3:17–21**: What are the consequences of remaining God's enemy? Do we share the grief Paul feels on their behalf?
* **1 Timothy 2:1–6**: Whom are we being asked to pray for? Why is God pleased by such prayers?

QUESTIONS FOR YOUNGER LISTENERS

* What terrible thing did the squirrel do?
* Why did Tuppenny ask the otter to rescue the squirrel?
* What was the warning the otter gave the squirrel?
* Why does Jesus tell us to pray for our enemies?

VISUAL AIDS AND ACTIONS

* A recorder

Ask someone to play 'Pop goes the weasel' on a recorder or other instrument.

WALKING THE TIGHTROPE

'When someone tries to eat you,' said Mrs Hedgehog, 'you have to roll up in a ball and stick all your spines out, like this.' And she did.

'I can't do it,' said Eli.

'Except cars. Don't roll up for cars,' said Mrs Hedgehog. 'Run.' And she did.

'I can't do it,' said Eli, and he hobbled forward a bit, after his mother. She sighed and Eli wandered off, looking for something to eat. He saw a robin sitting on a branch with a large worm in her beak.

'Gulp!' she went. 'You have to be sharp-eyed to catch a worm.'

'I can't do it,' said Eli.

The robin finished the worm and then began to sing clear, beautiful notes. Eli listened. 'I wish I could sing,' he said to himself. 'But I can't.'

He came to the riverbank and watched the ducks bobbing on the water. One of them up-tailed and its head disappeared. It came up again eating a long trail of green weeds.

'Swimming looks fun,' thought Eli. 'But I can't do it.'

A few drops of rain began to fall, and Eli huddled in the reeds for shelter. 'Urrr!' croaked a frog next to him. Its long tongue suddenly shot out and stuck to a passing fly. The fly disappeared into the frog's mouth. 'I'm glad I can't do that!' said Eli.

When the rain stopped, he walked on through the woods and then saw the strangest sight he'd ever seen. A hare was walking across a rope tied between two trees. Eli stared and stared. When the hare got halfway across, he stopped, took out three apples and began to juggle with them. As he caught the last one, he looked round and saw Eli watching him.

'Bet you can't do that,' said the hare.

'I bet I can!' said Eli.

'Oh, can you?' The hare jumped down on to the ground. 'Go on, then.'

Eli felt a bit silly. He sniffed at the rope and reached out a front paw to touch it. The rope swung away from him, and he stepped back in surprise.

'You see,' said the hare. 'It's not so easy. It's taken me years of practice.'

'Will you teach me?' asked Eli.

Hedgehogs aren't made the same way as hares. There were some things Eli could never do. But the hare was willing to teach him different tricks. Every day Eli went into the woods to practise, and the hare was a very good teacher.

Whenever Eli said, 'I can't do it,' the hare would say, 'Nobody can, till they learn—and nobody can learn till they are willing. Are you willing?'

'Yes,' said Eli.

So Eli learnt to walk a tightrope, very slowly and carefully. He also learnt to roll up in a ball and roll from one end of the rope to the other, while the hare jumped over him. They put on a show in the woods, and all the animals came to watch them and clapped and cheered at the end.

'I can't believe it's you, Eli!' said his cousin Bryony. 'I thought you couldn't do anything.'

'I couldn't,' said Eli. 'Nobody can, till they learn.'

So follow my example. PHILIPPIANS 4:9

BIBLE REFERENCES

Deuteronomy 6:4–9; John 13:12–17; John 14:25–26; Philippians 4:8–9

SERMON POINTERS

* **Deuteronomy 6:4–9**: Are these instructions just about learning rules, or something deeper? In what way are they relational?
* **John 13:12–17**: What teaching methods did Jesus use? How do we learn best?
* **John 14:25–26**: How is the teaching of Jesus to continue? Are we aware of the Holy Spirit teaching us as a church, and as individuals?
* **Philippians 4:8–9**: How does Paul teach? Whose example do you follow today? Do we think of this when we talk of 'good teaching'?

QUESTIONS FOR YOUNGER LISTENERS

* What are the things Eli said he couldn't do?
* What are some of the things you have learnt to do?
* What did Eli learn to do?
* Who helped him? How did he help?
* How did Jesus help his disciples to learn?

VISUAL AIDS AND ACTIONS

* A rope

Lay the rope flat along the ground. See if the children can walk along it.

❖

THE BELLS

'I remember,' said Five, 'when the church was full.'

'So do I,' said Four.

'I remember when the village was full,' said Three.

'And the farms were working,' said Two. 'And the fields were full of people at harvest time.'

'I don't remember,' said One, who was the smallest.

'That's because you're new,' said Five. 'You've only been here seventy years.'

All the bells in the belfry nodded and their ropes shook.

'It's only a matter of time before we're sold off,' said Four.

'Or melted down,' said Three.

'I used to be a kettle,' said One. 'Till they melted me into a bell.'

'I wonder what they'll turn us into,' said Four.

'Something electronic,' said Five miserably.

The bells fell silent as they thought about the days when they rang out over the village green, and men, women and children would come hurrying to church. And there would be snow at Christmas, and spring flowers at Easter. But the village was empty now, just a few broken-down houses, and everyone moved to the nearby towns. The churchyard was neglected and overgrown, and the surrounding fields turned into pasture for sheep.

'Visitors,' whispered Four, as the latch lifted on the old wooden door. Two children and a woman walked in, followed by a man and a dog. The dog ran down the aisle, sniffing. One child sat on a pew, kicking her legs, and the other climbed into the pulpit.

'Nice wall painting,' said the man.

'It's cold in here. Damp and cold.' The woman shivered. 'Come on, let's go. It's going to rain.'

As they were leaving, one of the children looked up into the belfry. 'What's up there?' he asked.

'Bells,' said the man. 'They tell people to come to church.'

'Don't touch,' said the woman. 'Come on.'

The door closed behind them and the bells began to mutter.

'We don't tell people to come to church,' said Four. 'Not any more.'

'There's no one to tell,' said Three.

'People don't come,' said Two.

'We could try,' said One.

'Try?' said Five.

'Yes,' said One. 'We could ring ourselves.'

'It's not allowed,' said Five.

'Nobody would know it was us,' said One.

That night there was a storm. The wind shook the steeple and howled under the door, and the rain spread against the windows. At midnight, the bells began to rock backwards and forwards till they'd all swung high up into the air.

'Ready?' said Five. 'Off you go, One.'

A wonderful peal of bells rang out over the fields, mixing with the wind and rain and the crashing thunder. Some people far away thought it was only the wind. Others thought they were dreaming.

The message reached to the owls and badgers in the woods, and woke the sheep huddled under the swaying trees. 'Sing joy to the world,' sounded the bells. 'For Christ is risen. Rejoice and be glad. For Christ is risen.'

The next morning, the bells hung quietly together in the belfry.

'Whatever happens to us,' said Five, 'I know we've done something special. We've told the world that God is good, and there's reason to be happy.'

All the bells agreed that whatever happened to them, wherever they ended up, they would go on ringing, 'Sing joy to the world. For Christ is risen. Rejoice and be glad. For Christ is risen.'

Tell everyone on this earth to sing happy songs in praise of the Lord. PSALM 98:4

BIBLE REFERENCES

Psalm 98; Luke 9:1–6; Acts 16:22–34; 1 John 1:1–4

SERMON POINTERS

★ **Psalm 98**: Do our worship and our witness reflect the joy of this psalm? What reasons are given for rejoicing?

★ **Luke 9:1–6**: What was the good news that the disciples were to spread? What instructions did Jesus give them? Do any still apply to us?

★ **Acts 16:22–34**: How did Paul and Silas behave in jail? What did the jailer ask Paul and Silas? How did he and his family respond to the answer?

★ **1 John 1:1–4**: What has John seen that he must talk about? Why is he telling others? Why does it make him happy?

QUESTIONS FOR YOUNGER LISTENERS

★ Why did no one go to the church?

★ What message did the bells have to tell?

★ Why did they want to go on telling people?

★ What did Jesus tell his disciples to do?

★ How can we tell people about Jesus?

VISUAL AIDS AND ACTIONS

★ A collection of different bells, such as:
  • A handbell   • A doorbell
  • An alarm clock   • A cat bell

Ask the children what different bells, including church bells, are for.

THE CANDLE WHO LIVED UNDER THE STAIRS

This is a story about a large box of candles. They lived in the cupboard under the stairs. Some of them were very tall and thin, and some were short and round. Some had amazing patterns on them: one looked like a stained-glass window. Some had burnt for a long time and were smaller and stubbier than they used to be. The best ones left the cupboard on special occasions—birthdays and festivals. When they returned, they'd tell the others what a wonderful party it had been.

The candles knew that there was one time when they'd all be used. They'd hear a voice call, 'Power cut!' The cupboard door would open and the whole box would be grabbed. It didn't matter then if you were tall or short, old or new. As long as you shone in the dark, you were needed.

One cold, winter evening in January, the cupboard door opened and all the candles were removed. 'Power cut,' muttered Stumpy, the oldest—and he was put in his usual place by the front door.

'I'm on the windowsill this time,' called Drippy.

'Mind the curtains,' Stumpy called back. 'Where's Curly?'

'Here,' said Curly. 'They've put me on the radiator. It's still hot!'

But there was one candle who was new, and he wasn't sure he liked being a candle.

Sparky had always dreamed of being a firework, of soaring through the air and exploding in a thousand coloured sparks while people clapped and cheered. He was very grumpy at being dragged out and put at the top of the stairs.

In fact, he was so cross about it, he waited till he was alone, then he leaned forward as far as he could towards a draught and blew himself out.

'There,' he said. 'Why should I waste myself lighting a stupid staircase? I shall save myself for a much more important occasion.'

Sparky stood there in the dark, listening to the people downstairs wandering about.

Then he heard a bedroom door softly creaking open, and he could just make out a little child moving forward along the passageway. It was so dark that the child couldn't see the stairs, and she was heading straight for them.

'No!' cried Sparky. 'No! What have I done?'

He tried very hard to light himself but he couldn't. He couldn't even glow. 'Stop!' he shouted, but only the other candles heard him.

'What is it?' they called.

'I've gone out,' he told them, 'and there's a child heading for the stairs.'

Below him, the other candles shook and dribbled in horror. 'It's our job to light the house,' said Stumpy. 'This has never happened before.'

'It's all my fault,' wailed Sparky. 'What am I going to do?'

A second later, the power came back on. The little child sat down suddenly on the top step and laughed. Her mother ran up and caught her. 'What are you doing here, mischief?' she said. 'Come on, let's put the candles away.'

When they were all back in their box and the cupboard door was tightly shut, Sparky knew he had to tell them the truth. 'I blew myself out,' he said. Then he explained how he'd always wanted to be a firework, and how angry he'd been just to be stuck on a staircase, and how awful he felt. There was a long pause.

'I fell into a box of fireworks once,' said Drippy. 'I set off two rockets and a catherine wheel.'

Sparky began to feel better. He promised himself that if he was ever used in a power cut again, he'd shine as brightly as he could for as long as he could. He'd learnt that a blown-out candle is no use to anyone.

> **Try to shine as lights among the people of this world.**
> PHILIPPIANS 2:15

BIBLE REFERENCES

Isaiah 60:1–3; Matthew 5:13–16; Acts 13:44–47;
Philippians 2:14–16

SERMON POINTERS

* **Isaiah 60:1–3**: What is the light shining in Jerusalem? Who is reached by it?
* **Matthew 5:13–16**: What is the warning here for the disciples? And what is their role? What is the light that Jesus speaks of?
* **Acts 13:44–47**: What was the ministry that God gave Paul and Barnabas? Why are they described as a light? What light do we bring?
* **Philippians 2:14–16**: How can we keep shining in a dark world? What do we need to help us? How can we be of help to each other?

QUESTIONS FOR YOUNGER LISTENERS

* Why was Sparky's job so important?
* Do you think Sparky was being selfish?
* Do you think he knew what an important job he'd been given?
* What job has Jesus given us to do?
* How can Christians keep their light shining?

VISUAL AIDS AND ACTIONS

✶ A collection of different candles such as:
  - A church candle
  - A tealight
  - A floating candle
  - A decorative candle
  - A Pascal candle

Ask the children why each candle might be used.

✢

THE STATUE

There was a time when kings were very powerful and could order people to do almost anything. Some kings kept a court jester—a kind of clown—to remind them that they were only human and could make mistakes. The jester would tell jokes and stories to show the king when he was being foolish or unfair. It wasn't an easy job. Sometimes a king could get very angry and the jester would end up in prison—or worse.

Once there was a king who was a good man and who tried to rule his people fairly. But then he grew so powerful that he had a great statue of himself made and put in the courtyard. He was very proud of the statue and daily watched from the window as people passed it by. When they stopped to look at it, he imagined them admiring him and saying what a great king he was.

'It is a wonderful statue of me,' he sighed. But the jester said nothing.

As time went by, the king felt how nice it would be if people got into the habit of admiring him properly. So he called the palace guard to his chamber. 'I want people to show *more* respect as they pass my statue. I want them to pause, and bow.'

'Yes, your Majesty,' said the guards. But the jester said nothing.

The king kept watch from the window and enjoyed seeing people bow to his statue. He was rather annoyed, though, when a group passed by chatting so much that they forgot.

'I have made another rule,' said the king. 'There will be silence as people cross the courtyard, and when they reach the statue they must shout, 'Long live the king!'

'Yes, your Majesty,' said the guards. But the jester said nothing.

Then the king noticed that people were not as fond of him as before. They thought him stern and cruel, and they grew afraid of him.

One day, the king glanced out of the window and saw a crowd

gathering in the courtyard. There, clutching the legs of the statue and weeping aloud, was the jester.

'My king has turned to stone,' he cried. 'Look, oh people. See how hard and cold he is. He will not even turn to look at me. Oh, what has happened to him? A king made of stone!' And the jester wept real tears.

The king strode into the courtyard, annoyed and alarmed. 'Jester, what is this nonsense?' he demanded. 'I am the king, not this stone statue.'

The jester leapt to his feet and bowed, and his face cleared. 'A miracle!' he cried. 'Your Majesty is human again.'

The king looked puzzled and quite angry, and then he began to laugh. 'You mischief!' he said. 'Is this what you would teach me? The statue is only a statue, and I am only a man. Very well, I will show you I have learnt my lesson.'

So the king had another statue made, this time of the jester. He had it placed next to his own statue, and the face of the jester was laughing. No one who passed by and saw the statue of the jester could quite be afraid of the king again. They even imagined that on the stern face of the king's statue a smile had begun to form.

Consider others more important than yourselves.
PHILIPPIANS 2:3

BIBLE REFERENCES

Daniel 4:28–32; Mark 9:33–37; Luke 14:7–11; Philippians 2:1–11

SERMON POINTERS

* **Daniel 4:28–32:** What lesson did Nebuchadnezzar have to learn? How might we fall into the same mistake?
* **Mark 9:33–37:** Do you think the disciples knew that their argument was inappropriate? Have we known similar arguments to take place in our churches?
* **Luke 14:7–11:** Is Jesus talking about good social behaviour or giving us an insight into the kingdom of God? How can we avoid thinking too much of ourselves?
* **Philippians 2:1–11:** What are the qualities that Paul would like to see in the Philippian church? How does he reason with them?

QUESTIONS FOR YOUNGER LISTENERS

* What job did the jester have to do?
* What effect did power have on the king?
* Did the jester really think the king had turned into a statue? What was he trying to say?
* What did Jesus teach his disciples about which of them was the most important?

VISUAL AIDS AND ACTIONS

* A jester's cap and bells

Ask one of the children to model the cap for the first paragraph of the story.

MAX THE MOTORBIKE

Maximilian was a sleek black motorbike. He was very proud of his glossy paintwork and shining chrome pipes and the purr of his powerful engine. He lived in a small village where people were not used to motorbikes, and he enjoyed very much knowing that people were watching him as he rode by. Children would wave and call out and wish that they could have a go riding him.

Max loved all the attention, but he didn't often have the chance to go out. His rider was too busy and was always sitting in her office at a computer, or going to work or to meetings, or stopping at friends' houses to talk to them. Max felt very important but he also felt very bored.

Being bored, he would dream of another place—a country of long, long roads and vast open plains. He would dream of petrol that lasted longer and tasted better, and always left his engine feeling cleaner—and of other motorbikes, thousands of them, who could never keep up with him and who were in awe of his splendour and strength.

One autumn day, it began to rain. It rained for hours. It rained for days. It looked as if it would rain for weeks. Many of the roads to the village were flooded. Some outlying houses were underwater, and farmers lost their crops and their livestock was in danger.

Max didn't like rain very much. But for some reason his rider went out more than usual, visiting friends whose homes were flooded, and even shopping for some people. Max couldn't believe he was being made to go shopping!

Early one morning, Max and his rider were out on a winding country road when they saw someone waving by the roadside. They slowed to a halt and a woman ran over to them.

'Two kids,' said the woman breathlessly, 'stuck on an island. The water's rising. We need a boat.'

'Have you phoned for help?'

'The lines are down. Have you got a mobile?'

'Not on me.'

The woman rubbed the rain off her face with both hands. 'There's a boat over at Gerry's farm,' she said. 'Can you get over there and tell them to come quick?'

And that is how Max came to be riding, not very fast on a wonderful open road, but very slowly down muddy lanes, and across the top end of fields, and through shallow ditches. His glossy paint was completely covered in mud, his spokes were clogged and he was scratched by bushes and briars.

'I'm not a scrambler,' he wailed. 'I didn't dream of this!'

'Come on, Max,' urged his rider. 'Keep going.'

Max promptly slipped and slithered several yards down a bank, but then he was upright again and travelling on.

Soon they could see the farmhouse just ahead of them. They delivered their message, and within minutes the boat was hitched to a Landrover and being towed as fast as possible along the country lanes.

Max's rider swerved him round in a circle. 'OK, Max,' she said. 'Let's go back and make sure everything is all right.'

'No!' protested Max. 'It's not fair! I want to go home!'

But Max had to go through the whole muddy journey all over again. This time they rode to the edge of the floodwater. Then they stood and watched as the two children climbed into the boat and were rowed to safety. Max saw the woman run down to the boat and hold them in her arms. He began to feel different. He realized that he no longer felt bored, and that something better than his daydream had happened.

He still felt proud of his speed and his strength and his skill, but in a new way—not because they made him feel important but because they'd helped him do something that was really worth doing.

> **If you love the world, you cannot love the Father.** 1 JOHN 2:15

BIBLE REFERENCES

Proverbs 29:23; Luke 16:14–15; Romans 12:1–5; 1 John 2:15–17

SERMON POINTERS

* **Proverbs 29:23**: What is the difference between pride and honour? How should we honour each other, ourselves and God?
* **Luke 16:14–15**: What was the fault of the Pharisees? Do we care too much for how we look in other people's eyes? How does God see us?
* **Romans 12:1–5**: How can we serve God with our bodies? How do we picture the body of Christ? Are we aware what role we have as part of Christ's body?
* **1 John 2:15–17**: Is this a call to reject the physical world? What does John mean by 'the world'? What foolish pride and selfish desires do we bring into our Christian lives?

QUESTIONS FOR YOUNGER LISTENERS

* How did Max feel about himself?
* Why didn't he want to help the children?
* What did he learn about himself in the end?
* What sort of skills and gifts does God give us?
* How does he want us to use them?

VISUAL AIDS AND ACTIONS

✱ Borrow a biker's helmet and gloves.
✱ Better still, borrow the bike!

Talk about why a motorbike is different from any other vehicle. In what ways is it better; and in what ways is it worse?

❖

THE RAVEN AND THE DOVES

Once there lived a young king who was surrounded by powerful noblemen. Early one morning, as he rode out into the hills, the king looked up and saw a raven. Its great wings were stretched out like a cross, and it glided easily in the warm spring air. As he watched, it flipped over on to its back, and then upright again.

'Oh, to be a raven!' cried the king. 'To have such freedom! See how high he can fly.'

Just to show off, the raven mounted higher still and rolled over in the air before gliding away towards the mountains.

'Such power in his wings!' sighed the king. 'What strength!'

'It is a wonderful bird,' agreed his companions.

The young king murmured to himself, 'If only I had the power of the raven at my command. Then we would be the greatest kingdom on earth.'

The noblemen surrounding the king smiled at each other, for they too dreamed of having such power.

The king rode home and spent the day signing papers and discussing affairs of state. Towards evening, he yawned and walked out into his garden. A flock of doves were nesting in the garden wall, bustling and cooing, and picking seeds from the ground. Some children were playing nearby, and the doves pecked around their feet and made them laugh. One young girl knelt down, and a dove reached out its neck and took seed from the palm of her hand.

The king thought of the raven. 'What useless birds you are,' he said to the doves. 'You are no more than pretty toys.' And he kicked at one angrily. It dodged away and carried on eating.

But that night the king had a dream, and it was a savage dream. He dreamed that the ravens came to the garden and carried away the doves, and there was nothing but feathers left on the grass and broken eggs in the nest. Without the doves, it seemed as if the garden were full of shadows.

The next day, as usual, the king met with his noblemen. As he listened, he suddenly grew tired of hearing them quarrelling among themselves and wanting more power.

He dismissed them and called back one elderly man who had been a councillor in his father's day.

'Tell me,' said the king, 'is it better to have the power of the raven or the gentleness of a dove?'

The man thought for a moment and then he replied, 'It is better that the power of the raven serve the dove than the dove serve the raven.'

The young king looked up at him. 'You are right,' he said. 'I would not want a kingdom where the ravens rule.'

So he made the elderly man his chief councillor. He still loved to go up into the hills and watch the ravens soaring and diving, but he kept the doves in his palace grounds to remind him that a king's power is given to him so that he might serve.

> **'The good shepherd gives up his life for his sheep.'**
> JOHN 10:11

BIBLE REFERENCES

Psalm 74:18–21; Luke 3:21–22; John 10:11–13; Galatians 5:13–15

SERMON POINTERS

✴ **Psalm 74:18–21:** Who are the helpless in today's world? How can we use our strength to defend them?

✴ **Luke 3:21–22:** What does the image of the Holy Spirit as a dove say to us? Does it seem a weak image? The doves of the Bible would not have been white: does this change our perception of these verses?

* **John 10:11–13**: How and why does the good shepherd guard the flock? Who are the hired workers spoken of in these verses? In what way does Jesus protect us today?
* **Galatians 5:13–15**: What is the freedom that Paul speaks of, and how can we use it to serve each other? How can we guard against the tendency to attack each other?

QUESTIONS FOR YOUNGER LISTENERS

* What did the king like about the raven?
* What did the king learn from the doves?
* How did Jesus use his power during his life on earth?
* What power do we have? How should we use it?

VISUAL AIDS AND ACTIONS

* Sheets of drawing paper
* Scissors
* String

Cut out shapes of ravens and doves. Attach them to pieces of string.

THE MONKEY'S SERVANT

Once the great river flooded and the animals had to flee their homes. The monkey gathered all his belongings together and tried to carry them, but he had too many and they were too heavy.

A donkey was walking by, carrying nothing but a bale of hay. Before she knew what was happening, the monkey had heaped all his belongings on top of her, till she could hardly stand. He himself carried nothing but swaggered forward very proudly. 'I have a donkey to carry my things,' he told the other animals. 'I see you have to carry your own.'

The donkey tried her best, but occasionally she stumbled. Then the monkey would beat her with a stick and say, 'Come on, you lazy creature. Keep moving!' He was a horrid monkey.

Now there was a rumour among the animals that the lion, the king of beasts, was going to join them on the highway. The monkey was very pleased. 'Good to have some quality around,' he said. 'These other animals are very dull.' He imagined how the lion might notice him among the rest and walk beside him. They would talk together of important things, and the lion would be impressed with the monkey's clever ways.

It was a pleasant thought, and the monkey smiled to himself as he walked along.

Then, suddenly, to his great rage, he noticed the donkey trotting past, carrying nothing at all. She was prancing along as free as a bird.

'You rogue!' called the monkey. 'What have you done with my things? You wait till I catch you.'

But the donkey carried on, and the monkey saw the other animals looking at him in a strange way. Nervously, he glanced back over his shoulder. There was the lion walking slowly along, carrying all the monkey's belongings, and perched on top was the donkey's bale of hay.

The monkey was horrified and froze to the spot. The lion came up to him and gave a great shake, and all the monkey's bags and suitcases dropped to the ground. 'I believe these are yours,' growled the lion, and walked on.

The monkey felt very ashamed and he crawled forward with his head bent. He didn't know whether to pick up all his things and try to carry them, or to leave them where they were and run after the lion. Meanwhile, the lion walked on with the donkey—the lion carrying the hay and the donkey dancing.

> **'You cheat people, and you don't love God.'** LUKE 11:42

BIBLE REFERENCES

Amos 2:6–8; Matthew 11:27–30; Luke 11:42–46; 1 Thessalonians 2:1–12

SERMON POINTERS

* ✶ **Amos 2:6–8**: Why does God judge Israel to have sinned? How are religious and social behaviour linked? Do we link the two, or tend to separate them in our teaching?
* ✶ **Matthew 11:27–30**: What sort of burdens is Jesus talking about? What does he mean by his 'yoke'? How is this linked with knowing the Father?
* ✶ **Luke 11:42–46**: What criticisms does Jesus have of the Pharisees and teachers of the law? What do we learn from these verses about God's values?
* ✶ **1 Thessalonians 2:1–12**: What motives does Paul discuss for his work among the Thessalonians? How has he refused to burden them? Are we careful not to take advantage of people because of our power or position?

QUESTIONS FOR YOUNGER LISTENERS

* How did the monkey treat the donkey?
* What could the monkey have done instead?
* Why did the lion carry the donkey's load?
* What kind of problems do people have that might load them down?
* How does Jesus promise to help them?

VISUAL AIDS AND ACTIONS

* Bags and suitcases

Struggle in, carrying an armful of bags and suitcases. You might ask for help from the children.

···

THE GAZELLE

A tiger came out of the forest towards a gazelle, tethered by her leg to a tree. She was tugging at the rope and struggling. He stalked forward, crouched, and was about to spring.

'Stop!' cried the gazelle. 'Before you leap, you should know something.'

'What?' said the tiger.

'I am stronger than you.'

'Oh?' laughed the tiger. 'How can that be?'

'Because if you leap, you will catch a gazelle. But I will catch a tiger.'

The tiger paused. He wasn't used to this sort of conversation. 'Explain yourself,' he said.

'Hidden in the tree above me,' said the gazelle, 'is a large net. There are men a short distance away. They are ready to drop the net on you when you come near enough—and then they will sell you to a zoo.'

The tiger thought about this. He was hungry, but not so hungry that he wanted to take the risk. He turned and walked away.

After a time, the men gave up waiting for the tiger and let the gazelle go free. She ran back to her friends and they greeted her warmly. But she had changed. She was so proud of herself for outwitting the tiger that she began to think she was greater than everyone else.

'I am stronger and cleverer than any of you,' she said. 'I am stronger than the tiger who stalks the forest. You should make me your leader.'

The other gazelles didn't much like the idea, but they agreed, and so she became their leader. She was hard to please and very bossy, and when the tiger came hunting she demanded that everyone else protect her.

'She ought to be protecting us, if she's so clever,' whispered one gazelle.

'Ssh!' said her neighbour. 'Don't let her hear you. She may send you away.'

There was nothing worse for a gazelle than to be sent away from the herd to live alone.

Time passed, and the gazelles began to complain about their leader in secret, down by the river's edge. The river listened, and when she came down to drink, the river lapped at her hooves, and spoke to her. 'Why should I let you drink?'

The gazelle looked at the water in surprise. 'Because I choose to,' she said.

'No, I choose,' said the river. 'I could send a great flood and sweep you away in a moment. Or I could move away from the forest, and you would die of thirst.'

The gazelle backed away slightly. But then she remembered. 'I am stronger than the tiger,' she said proudly.

'Oh, so am I,' said the river. 'And yet I let the tiger drink as well as you. It is not because you are strong that I let you drink. It is because you are thirsty.'

The gazelle didn't know what to do. She didn't like the river very much any more, but she was terribly thirsty. At last she humbly bent her head and began to drink.

And as she drank, the river whispered to her, 'Remember this, if you wish to lead. Good leaders use their power to help others. Bad leaders use others to bring them power. Which are you?'

The gazelle thought and thought. She knew she was clever, she knew she was brave, and deep down she knew she wanted to be a good leader, like the river.

So she went back to the other gazelles with the river's words in her mind, and they could tell by her face that things were going to be different.

Don't be bossy to those people who are in your care.
1 PETER 5:3

BIBLE REFERENCES

1 Kings 3:5–14; Matthew 20:25–28; 1 Corinthians 3:4–9;
1 Peter 5:1–4

SERMON POINTERS

* **1 Kings 3:5–14**: What attitude to power does Solomon reveal by his request? In what terms does he see his kingship?
* **Matthew 20:25–28**: How does Jesus view leadership? How does he demonstrate it?
* **1 Corinthians 3:4–9**: What lesson is Paul giving the Corinthians? How does he describe his own leadership? How can we apply this lesson to our own churches?
* **1 Peter 5:1–4**: How are church leaders to behave? What is to be their motivation? Who is to be their example?

QUESTIONS FOR YOUNGER LISTENERS

* Why did the gazelle think she was so important?
* How did she behave towards the other gazelles?
* What did the river teach her?
* How do you think she changed after that?
* What sort of leader was Jesus to his disciples?

VISUAL AIDS AND ACTIONS

* A rope

Do a tug-of-war with the children, as a test of strength.

❖

THE GOLD COINS

Jason and Tim had discovered their grandfather's old typewriter. It was huge and very heavy, and the keys had to be pushed down hard to type a letter.

'Where do you switch it on?' asked Jason.

'You don't,' said their sister, Katie.

'Does it have a spell-check?' asked Tim.

'No,' said Katie. 'You have to look words up in a dictionary.'

'What about games?' Jason peered into the depths of the machine. 'Does it have games on it?'

'No!' said Katie. 'It isn't a computer. It doesn't have a brain. You have to use your own brain.'

'It must be very old,' said Tim.

'Can I have a go?' asked Jason.

He rolled a piece of paper into the typewriter and pushed down a few keys. They all jammed together before they hit the paper.

The door opened and their grandmother came in. 'Let me show you,' she said. With slow fingers she pressed down the keys one by one and typed the words, 'Once upon a time…'

'There you are,' she told them. 'Some of the oldest words in the world.'

'Are you writing a story?' asked Jason.

'No, my fingers are not so strong. I shall tell you one instead, if you like.'

She sat down in an armchair and placed a cushion behind her back. Jason sat on the windowsill and Tim stood by the table, fiddling with the typewriter. Their grandmother began:

'Once upon a time, there was a man who wanted to hide his store of gold. He did not want to hide it in the ground or put it in the bank. He wanted to hide it in places where it could be found…'

'That's not hiding!' said Tim.

'Sshh!' said Katie.

'So he took his treasure and, piece by piece, he hid it. He wore one piece as a button on his coat, two more as buckles to his shoes. A handful he flung into the sky among the stars. Some he turned into flowers, and some he placed between the pages of a book.

'He took a loaf of bread and filled the centre with gold. He placed gold pieces among the pebbles in a stream. Still more he hid in the stories he told, and the rest he hid in acts of kindness and love.

'Then he set out to tell people that his treasure could be theirs. Not all were interested. They thought he was telling lies. At best they could only see one piece of gold, and they did not believe that there were more. Others followed him, though, and gradually they found more and more pieces, till they themselves grew rich.'

The old lady's voice ended, and there was a pause.

'Is it a true story?' asked Tim.

'It's a story about truth,' she replied.

'Why did he hide his gold?' asked Katie.

'So that only the people who really believed him would find it,' her grandmother said.

'Can *we* find it?' asked Jason.

'Yes. If you start looking.'

'Where do we look?' asked Tim.

Their grandmother looked at the eager faces around her and smiled. 'It seems to me, you have already found the first piece,' she said.

Search for wisdom as you would search for silver or hidden treasure. PROVERBS 2:4

BIBLE REFERENCES

Proverbs 2:1–5; Matthew 13:10–17; Ephesians 3:7–13;
1 Peter 1:8–12

SERMON POINTERS

* **Proverbs 2:1–5:** Do we hunger for wisdom and search for it as treasure? How may wisdom be known to us today?
* **Matthew 13:10–17:** What is the connection between stories and seeing? What could the disciples see that others could not?
* **Ephesians 3:7–13:** What was God's mysterious plan? How can we help everyone to understand? How does Christ help us?
* **1 Peter 1:8–12:** What did the prophets' searching reveal to them? How can we encourage other people to discover who Christ is?

QUESTIONS FOR YOUNGER LISTENERS

* Who told the children a story?
* What was it about?
* Why did the man hide his treasure?
* What did Jesus tell stories about?
* What did Jesus tell us to search for?

VISUAL AIDS AND ACTIONS

* Chocolate gold coins

Hide the coins around the room for the children to find.

❖

THE POTTER

Once there was a humble potter who lived in the palace of a great and powerful king. The king was very fussy about what he liked. He wanted all his pottery the same as it had always been—very heavy and plain and dull—and what the king didn't like, he would smash. The potter was very careful to do just as the king said. He always made the same plates, cups, saucers, jugs and bowls, day after day.

The potter hated working for the king, and he became pale and unhappy. He longed to be free to make his own pottery. But then one day something strange began to happen. As the potter worked the clay, he found his hands shaping the kind of pottery he loved. There were wonderful curving vases, and deep sturdy pots. Dishes that made you feel hungry just to look at them. Bowls the perfect size for holding in two hands, and funny, chunky mugs that made you want to laugh.

Each time the potter noticed it happening, he would squash the clay back down and start again. He was very nervous that a piece would end up on the king's table, and the king would send him to the dungeons. But still, he couldn't help himself—the clay kept forming into new shapes.

The potter discovered that the best thing to do was to make one piece of his own pottery every day. This he would hide in a great wooden trunk in his workshop. Then, for the rest of the day, the clay would behave itself.

The potter began to enjoy his work for the first time. While he made the king's pots, he thought about all his special treasures hidden in the trunk, and his heart grew lighter.

One day, the king decided to hold a great feast. He invited many important people from throughout the kingdom. Privately they thought the king was a cruel man, but they wanted to stay in his favour.

The day of the feast came, and the servants set the table, everything shining and polished. But then disaster struck. A young serving boy, who was new to the palace, tripped over a rug and, being small, he flew into the air and landed on the table. The table was so shiny that he shot from one end to the other, scattering plates and jugs and knives and forks everywhere. He landed on the floor the other end, ran out of the door, out of the palace, and did not stop till he had escaped from the king for ever.

Everywhere there was broken pottery. The servants were so frightened that they ran to the potter's workroom to bring back every piece of pottery they could find. It was not long before they opened the trunk of secret pieces. They were amazed and astonished at what they saw, and soon the table was set again with the new pottery.

When the king entered with his guests, he took one look at the table and his face became dark with rage. But something happened during the feast. The guests seemed to be more friendly with each other, more at ease. Some of them felt a heavy burden lift from their hearts, though they couldn't explain why. They also grew braver and bolder. They warned the king that he could not go on as before, that he had to consider other people as well.

Next day, the potter was summoned to the king. 'My guests liked your pottery so much that I gave it to them. Make me some more—lots more.'

So the potter was allowed to go on making his special pots, and the palace became a happier place. And the potter's work spread not only throughout the kingdom but throughout the whole world.

God thinks of us as a perfume that brings Christ to everyone. 2 CORINTHIANS 2:15

BIBLE REFERENCES

Exodus 31:1–6; Matthew 13:31–33; Acts 18:1–4;
2 Corinthians 2:14–17

SERMON POINTERS

✶ **Exodus 31:1–6:** How do artists and craftsmen reflect the Spirit of God? What place does art have in worship in your church?

✶ **Matthew 13:31–33:** How is the kingdom of God increased? What do we learn from these images that Jesus uses?

✶ **Acts 18:1–4:** Why did Paul, Aquila and Priscilla work together? What might have grown between them during this time? How do we use our skills to serve God's kingdom?

✶ **2 Corinthians 2:14–17:** Do we feel despondent at times that we make so little impact for Christ? What image do these verses give, and how do they encourage us?

QUESTIONS FOR YOUNGER LISTENERS

✶ Why were people afraid of the king?

✶ What did the potter find was happening to his clay?

✶ What made the king change his mind about the potter's work?

✶ How do you think God would like you to use your skills and talents?

VISUAL AIDS AND ACTIONS

✶ A selection of hand-thrown pots or an original painting

Introduce an artist from your congregation. Ask them to share their work and their faith.

BIBLE INDEX

OLD TESTAMENT

STORIES TO MAKE YOU THINK

HEATHER BUTLER

Sensitive and topical issues approached through imaginative stories for 6–10s. Relevant Bible passages, thinking time, prayers and suggestions for further discussion are included with each story.

Topics covered include bereavement, bullying, self-value, being scared, racial issues, gender issues and making friends.

ISBN 1 84101 034 0 £5.99

FURTHER STORIES TO MAKE YOU THINK

HEATHER BUTLER

More sensitive and topical issues approached through imaginative stories, along with Bible passages, thinking time, prayers and suggestions for further discussion.

Topics covered include fairness, setting simple goals, looking after living things, how the media present information, peer pressure, stranger danger and living with separated parents.

ISBN 1 84101 202 5 £5.99

Available from your local Christian bookshop or, in case of difficulty, using the order form on page 175.

STORIES TO READ ALOUD

50 Bible stories for assemblies,
RE and all-age worship

PATRICK COGHLAN

This book offers you fifty 'easy-listening' Bible stories in contemporary language for you to read aloud to children, starting with Genesis and finishing with Acts. Each story has been skilfully written to reflect the original Bible story, and delightfully constructed to add interest and insight to the original text.

The pick-up-and-use formula is ideal for assemblies and RE in schools, but equally accessible for church-based worship and tecaching.

Each story is accompanied by its Bible reference, with the key verse written in full and a 'jigsaw piece' giving information on how the story fits into the overall picture.

ISBN 1 84101 362 5   £15.99

Available from your local Christian bookshop or, in case of difficulty, using the order form on page 175.

❧ barnabas

Resourcing children's work in church and school

Simply go to **www.brf.org.uk** and visit the barnabas pages

BRF is a Registered Charity

A Browse our books and buy online in our **bookshop**.

B In the **forum**, join discussions with friends and experts in children's work. Chat through the problems we all face, issues facing children's workers, where-do-I-find… questions and more.

C **Free** easy-to-use downloadable **ideas** for children's workers and teachers. Ideas include:
  - Getting going with prayer
  - Getting going with drama
  - Getting going with the Bible… and much more!

D In **The Big Picture**, you'll find short fun reports on Barnabas training events, days we've spent in schools and churches, as well as expertise from our authors, and other useful articles.

E In the section on **Godly Play**, you'll find a general introduction and ideas on how to get started with this exciting new approach to Christian education.